Cowboy Missionary in Kwangsi

# Cowboy Missionary in Kwangsi

**REX RAY**

BROADMAN PRESS · Nashville, Tennessee

DEWEY DECIMAL CLASSIFICATION: 266.092

*Library of Congress catalog card number: 64–24025*

Printed in the United States of America

1.5AL67KSP

# Acknowledgments

Members of the Rex Ray family wish to thank Mrs. Ruby Witherspoon, who typed the original copy of the manuscript, and Mrs. Marie Chapman, who edited it for the family.

MRS. LOIS RAY MCKENZIE

# Prologue

The blockade-running missionary, Rex Ray, was "what he had been becoming" throughout a childhood and youth in a courageous pioneer family in north central Texas. Born November 11, 1885, the eldest of the children of Hez F. and Mary Dee Reeves Ray, young Rex learned at eleven to "put his hand to the plow without looking back." Wagonloads of corn put into the crib from his field taught him the laws of sowing and reaping.

There was early evidence, too, of the persistence which later was to keep the missionary going when all odds were against him. Even the old swimming hole proved to be a training point. The boy, who one day would cross oceans aboard steamships, became acquainted with dangerous waters when, with his father, he forded the rolling, swirling Red River on hunting trips.

The future missionary learned well, too, that duties and responsibilities go on, "come wind, come weather." After the family moved to the ranch in Indian territory, there were cows to be milked. So in the dead of winter, with aching feet and numb fingers, he milked equally uncomfortable cows—

the effort resulting in smashed milk pails, spilled milk, and exploding tempers of both boy and cow.

When he was twelve, breaking a wild horse was a sum- mer afternoon's sport. With the aid of his younger brothers, Rex corraled and saddled the handsome black four year old —nine hundred pounds of wild horse flesh. He rode the bronc, which cowhands later declared was "the hardest horse they ever broke."

One of the youth's quieter pastimes led to permanent re- cording of thrilling missionary adventures. Young Rex Ray invested thirty-five cents for a camera and developing outfit from a mail-order house. Even color motion pictures he later made could not compare with the thrills of that early investment.

He was fifteen when his healthy forty-five-year-old father told him, "If anything should ever happen to me . . . take good care of your mother and help her care for your brothers and sisters." A week later, his father had crossed the great divide. He died from blood poisoning.

There ensued a rugged winter when, with the help of a cousin, the Ray boys looked after the cattle on one thousand acres of land. While the mother and younger children stayed at the ranch, the "hands" lived in a tent near where they kept cows with calves, yearlings, and ailing animals. During one blizzard, even the cookfire had to be built under the tent. Rex fried bacon by holding a skillet over the low fire. He lay flat on the ground to escape the smoke. After breakfast, wagonloads of corn and hay had to be taken to herds of cattle at points all over the range.

After the family moved back to Texas, the mother could keep her boys and girls in church as well as in school. But young Rex was not attracted to worship services by any sense of devotion to God's house. He and other young swains knew that here they would see the lovely daughters of other farmers. They even sang in the choir in order to be near the fair ones.

When Rex Ray left home in January, 1905, to enrol in Tyler Commercial College to study bookkeeping and stenography, he was still not a Christian. The Methodist revival came and went, but Rex put off all who showed concern for his soul. He promised himself he would take that important step during the Baptist meeting. In the very last service he kept that promise.

Business diploma in hand, he went to work for a lumber company, at first, actually doing construction work. This, too, was part of the mold. Then he became a yardman. By the age of twenty-two he was managing a company yard.

About this time he conducted his first prayer meeting and was so frightened that his New Testament page blurred. He became Sunday school treasurer, church janitor, and ran the artificial gas plant which provided lights for the church.

His pastor at the Baptist church in Munday prayed that God would call someone from that church to serve in a special way. Rex had a strong suspicion which one God wanted to call, but argued that he would stay home and be a successful businessman and help finance other young people who could go as missionaries. This did not work. He spent one week going into the cornfields each night to pray. The following Sunday he answered God's call. Shortly thereafter he resigned from the lumber company and enrolled at Decatur Baptist College, where he was not too proud to push a broom over the college floors, milk cows, dig holes for setting out trees, or run the college waterworks. Later he was "straw boss" of the rebuilding of a burned-down dormitory. There were times when the pasteboard soles of his shoes wore thin and he could not even afford a two-cent stamp to mail a letter home.

One night in Decatur, through the words of Missionary

W. B. Glass, he heard the call to China. More years of preparation followed, this time at Baylor University, Waco, Texas.

Upon graduation in 1917, Rex Ray joined the U. S. Army as a chaplain. This sent him across the Atlantic Ocean on ocean transport duty. Although he was seasick from the U. S. A. to France, he preached to the soldiers aboard.

At the close of this service, en route home, he stopped at Richmond, Virginia, where Dr. T. B. Ray told him that on September 9, 1919, he had been appointed a missionary to China. Rex had a few months at home on his mother's farm before receiving the telegram from the Foreign Mission Board: "Sail from Seattle on March 1, 1920."

THE EDITOR

# Contents

Cowboy Missionary in Kwangsi

# 1
# Rookie Missionary

I must have looked as "green" as I felt the day I landed in Hong Kong. There I was, face to face with hordes of Chinese faces I had envisioned when the Lord first called me to be a missionary.

I sat down on my trunk and watched the strange scenes, as groups of people drifted by. I had all day, for the steamboat to Canton was not due to sail until that night. I looked again at the Chinese coolies who had met me. For moving my trunk, locker, and box of books—all my earthly possessions —to the steamer, they were staging a holdup. I repeated my price, and again they shook their heads. My patience outlasted theirs, however, for when at last they had my baggage safely aboard the steamer, I paid them *my* price, and they walked happily away.

In Canton I went ashore, not knowing one word of Chinese. Somehow the Lord led me through that bewildering heathen city, first in a ricksha and then by a sampan (a small boat).

When I arrived at the door of the mission and introduced myself to secretary-treasurer Dr. R. E. Chambers, he exclaimed,

"Why, how on earth did you get here by yourself? We didn't even know you were coming."

Language school was my first assignment. In front of me was a Chinese man who did not know a word of English, and I did not know one word of Chinese; yet this man was to teach me how to talk. I looked at him and he at me. He began hopping up and down like a flea on a hot stove. Each time he went up, he said *hei-shan*. Each time he went down, he said *tsoh*. I was supposed to have enough sense to understand by his antics and words that *hei-shan* meant get up and *tsoh* meant sit down.

After I had been in Canton about a month, I made an appointment to preach to the sailors on the Navy ship *Helena*. When I asked some Baptist missionary girls to go with me and help in the singing, Miss May Hine said, "I have a friend whose parents are Presbyterian missionaries. She is a soloist. How about bringing her along, too?"

"Fine. Suits me."

When I met this friend, Miss Janet Gilman, she was wearing a gorgeous fluffy blue hat and a sparkling white dress that made her—with her blond wavy hair and smiling blue eyes—look like an angel. I thought to myself, "Young lady, if no one already has a lien on you, you certainly are going to have trouble with a certain lanky Texan threatening to camp on your doorstep." She did not know, but I soon did, that she would sooner or later have to throw me out or take me in for keeps.

Janet told it on me through the years that I courted her with a book of poetry under one arm and the Bible under the other. Finally convinced that the Baptist position on baptism was right, she was accepted by the Tung Shan Baptist Church as a candidate for baptism, and I baptized her.

On November 11, 1920, in the little Presbyterian Chapel on the river front in Canton, before 150 of our friends—missionaries and business people—Dr. Fisher of the Presbyterian mission gave to me this angelic beauty to be my partner for life. Dr. Chambers, of the Baptist mission, performed a beautiful ceremony. The United States consul was there to set his official seal on our wedding certificiate. This made the contract legal.

A gay party awaited on the beautiful lawn of the girls' school. The wedding cake got lost on the ship between Hong Kong and Canton, but the bride's Chinese amah-cook had baked a lot of wonderful cakes. Our printed wedding invitations were lost also and did not show up until the guests were assembling for the wedding, so we gave them out as mementos.

Following the lawn party, Dr. and Mrs. Chambers spread for us a wonderful wedding supper at their home in Tung Shan of Canton.

We set out next day on our honeymoon via Hong Kong to Cheung Chow Island. In Hong Kong we just missed the last ferry, so we hired a small sampan and sailed happily out of the harbor for the honeymoon island. My bride started off our cruise by reading a book of exciting romance to her husband. But when the little vessel was well out to sea, a very naughty ocean began to toss our honeymoon bark about as if it were a ball. Ere long, my bride laid the book of romance aside and wilted like a flower on a hot day. About all the groom was interested in for the next several hours was solid land. We never went to sea again in so small a boat!

We spent part of our honeymoon on the island and then took off for the ancient city of Macao. There we visited the grave of the first Protestant missionary to China, Robert Morrison. Near his grave is that of Mrs. Ray's elder sister.

In February of 1921, we were called to Wuchow. Dr. R. E. Beddoe, medical missionary, was not only building the Stout Memorial Hospital and a residence for his family but was superintendent of both the boys and girls' schools. In addition, he was looking after the country evangelistic work, including seventeen preaching stations with Chinese preachers in charge. Because of eye trouble, a thorn in the flesh for more than forty years, Dr. Beddoe had to spend about a third of his time in total darkness.

We answered the call. Mrs. Ray's belongings—including household furniture—my two chairs, locker, a trunk, and box of books were loaded on an old stern-wheeler steamboat, and we sailed up West River to our new home. There, I became president of the boys' school, about which I knew absolutely nothing. As yet I could speak only a little Chinese. But the school was saved, and we carried on.

As a little girl, Janet spoke the Hainanese dialect, but now she had to learn Cantonese. So back in language school, we both continued to study.

After battling with Cantonese for two years, I left for my first missionary journey into the country. We fitted out the hospital motorboat and began the cruise up the river. With us were two Chinese evangelists, Wai Tung Peng and So One Teng.

After traveling 150 miles west of Wuchow, we anchored at Kwai Uen and hired horses to continue the journey. The Chinese brethren had insisted that the horses were large, so I consented to ride. Lo, when the mighty steeds were led out, their heads just barely stuck out from under the saddles in front and their tails from the rear! The Chinese preachers were small, so their horses were soon bobbing across the prairies, while my unfortunate horse was poking along far behind. As soon as the brethren were out of sight, I got off my steed and led him the rest of the way. Next day I walked and let the horse carry the baggage.

Our first night was spent in a village where there was only one Christian man. He was very happy to have us come to preach the gospel. Many of his neighbors came and listened earnestly. Long after bedtime men and boys remained, asking questions and examining my cot, mosquito net, and everything I had with me. We were all very happy that we had been permitted to bring the gospel to this village.

But the next morning all was changed. It seemed the devil had won the victory, for during the night our host's wife had died. A foreign-trained nurse there pronounced the woman dead. Our host was not only sad, because of his loss, but now his neighbors would say, "See, you let those Christians stay in your house last night, and you have been punished by having your wife taken from you."

We left So One Teng behind to conduct the funeral, while Wai Tung Peng and I continued on our way. That night when So One Teng caught up with us at the next town, his face was happy and his heart rejoicing. We marveled that he could come from a funeral in such a happy frame of mind. Then he explained. Just before they were ready to place the corpse in the coffin, the dead woman suddenly came to life and sat up in her bed. The husband was exceedingly happy. He had received his wife back from death and the devil had been defeated. Now his village would be all the more willing to hear the good news about his Saviour.

At the next town Brother Wai did the preaching. During the service a Chinese man came in and sat down beside me. Soon he turned to me and began talking, but I insisted that he listen to the sermon. I told him that after the service I would listen to what he had to say. He obeyed and listened, but first he called one of his servants to him and then sent him out. After the service we learned that for some time the man had been very sick. When he heard that a foreigner had come to town, he insisted that he be brought to the chapel. He said that, while he was sitting there beside me, his sickness had all gone away and he was cured. He wanted to thank me for healing him. We told him it was the Great Physician, Jesus Christ, who had healed him. This was our opportunity to tell him more about our Saviour. So our first missionary journey continued from village to village.

One day in Wuchow in 1922, the Communists decided to go on the warpath—just before dawn. Their plan was to murder all the leading Chinese citizens, including the missionaries. General Lui Oon Yim, a member of the Party and military commander in charge of Wuchow, was at the powwow. He persuaded the Reds to postpone their murder campaign for twenty-four hours. Then he sent his soldiers out over the city in groups of twenty. At a designated time they were to strike. By sunrise the next morning, instead of our being dead in our homes, the Communist leaders were all behind prison bars! This began a drive to put communism out of China. General Chiang Kai-shek heroically carried on the fight until the end of World War II, when he told General Marshall, "If the United States does not join in with me to finish driving communism out of China, it will not be long until your country will be fighting Red China." It was a sad day for America when she did not believe these prophetic words.

# 2

# Missionary to Bandits

In 1924, the walled city of Kweilin, with an army inside, was surrounded by another army. One of the Alliance missionaries had been killed, and one Baptist missionary had been reported killed also. Not a word had been heard from the missionaries in Kweilin for over three weeks, so we fitted out our boat with fuel for the round trip of more than four hundred miles. We loaded milk, food, and medical supplies for the beseiged missionaries and their families.

Our relief party consisted of R. A. Jaffray, Carnes, and Miller of the Christian and Missionary Alliance; two government officials; and our crew, representing Southern Baptists —altogether about twenty men. When we were halfway up the Foo River we came to the walled city of Chiu Ping. Here, government officials insisted on sending along eighty soldiers to protect us from bandits that were spreading terror throughout the Foo River district. The soldiers marched along the banks of the river as our seventy-five-foot motorboat struggled through 365 rapids between Wuchow and Kweilin.

Halfway between Chiu Ping and Ping Lok (the next city up the river), about 4:00 P.M. bandits opened fire on our boat. I was on the upper deck in the pilot house. As bullets whizzed all around us, I told the pilot to run the boat into a small sandbar on the side of the river near the soldiers and opposite the bandits. Our sailors threw out the anchor, jumped into the water beside the boat, and submerged themselves, with only their noses out of the water. I flopped down flat in the pilot house, folded up a cotton quilt, and put it between my head and the bullets. As I lay there waiting for the shooting to stop, I saw our brave soldiers going back over the mountains toward home and safety! The prospects of being captured were quite clear, but ways and means of escape were not.

Our crew of about twelve men were trembling and shaking, for they feared death, or maybe torture. Suddenly we saw our boat on fire. After having looted it, the bandits had poured on kerosene and set it on fire. But they had left behind our engineer and a boy who put out the fire and saved the boat. Shortly afterward the bandit chief came running up to me with some salve and bandages he had taken out of my medical supplies, asking me to bind up his burns. While setting the boat on fire, he had tangled with the gasoline and flames, and here he was—the fellow that had been shooting at me a few minutes before—begging me to treat his burns! I spread salve over his burns, then bandaged them the best I could.

I decided to ask a favor of him. I said, "Chief, you see all of these men of mine you have here. They are poor fellows that I hired in Wuchow to help run this boat. They will not be of any profit to you. You will just have to feed them. Why not just turn them loose and let them go back to our boat?"

He ordered his guards to turn them loose, but the guards hesitated because they wanted to use our men as pack horses to carry their loot back into the mountains. The chief jerked out his automatic pistol and said, "Turn them loose or I'll kill you!" The men were set free. But we were marched, single file on mountain trails, to a farmhouse, where we were

boosted up a ladder into the attic. There were Chinese prisoners who had been there until their beards had grown out. I
feared that we too might remain that long. I didn't mind
traveling through rocky mountains, crossing streams and rivers
day and night, but just to sit on the floor and wait for beards
to grow long wasn't my idea of a picnic! One of the bandits
brought me a can of milk and asked what it was. I borrowed
his dirk knife, punched two holes in the can, turned it up and
drank the contents, then told him, "That was milk,"
and handed him the empty can. Another bandit took Brother
Jaffray's eyeglasses and, sitting there before us, broke out the
lenses, remarking that he was going to make him a gold tooth
out of the frames.

We were glad when ordered to get on the march again.
A Chinese official on our boat, realizing that we would be
captured, threw away his fine clothes and dressed as a coolie.
But when the bandits saw his soft white hands and no humps
on his shoulders, they knew he was a rich man or an official.
They put thirty one-pound tins of evaporated milk in a sack,
then tied the sack of milk around his neck, and tied his arms
behind his back. He really had rough mountain climbing.

After midnight we stopped to eat a bit of hot rice. We
asked the bandits, "Now that you have us, what are your
plans?" They said, "We are going to get one hundred thousand dollars for you from the American and British governments."

"Too much money. Nobody is going to pay you that much
for a bunch of preachers," we said. They decided to send
Brother Jaffray to get the money. We told them, "He is a
Britisher. You will have to send along an American, too, if
you want to get any money out of America." They fell for
the suggestion.

Dr. Miller (of New York) and I talked it over. We decided
that I should remain, while he went along with Brother Jaffray

to freedom. Brother Carnes (of Australia) and I were held to stand good for the money. They left, and we took off up the canyons toward the mountain peaks. After an all-night climb through tropical jungles, we reached the summit at sunrise.

That day as our march continued down and up the mountains, our Chinese official kept throwing himself down beside the road as though he were all in. I saw a chance to whisper to him, "I have a plan to help you. When we get into camp you wait on me as though you were my servant. You will better impress the bandits that you are just a working man." He saw the point and said, "I'll do it." When we were put into a farmhouse later, my "servant" got an old fan and fanned me good. When cooking time came around, he always went to the cooking place and rustled the nicest bits of food for me. He played the part so well for the three weeks I was with the bandits that I think they were convinced he was, after all, just a servant for the foreigner. In the end he only had to pay two hundred dollars for his freedom.

About the second day, the bandit chief told us that he had some bad news: on the way to freedom, Brother Jaffray and Dr. Miller were captured by pirates. So our chief had to take us (because his gang of bandits was weaker than the others) to join the bad ones on a midnight march.

New plans had to be made as the big, bad pirate chief took over our little bandit chief and his prisoners. That night the big chief commanded all the bandits to sit down, "while this foreign devil (Brother Jaffray) preaches to us." Many men and women heard. There were prisoners who were waiting for death to deliver them from the terrible life they were compelled to live. We decided the Lord had permitted us to be missionaries to those bandits, for they might never have another opportunity to hear how to be saved.

When the bandits first took us they threatened to make hash of us unless our friends soon put up the one hundred thousand dollars. We told them we could do nothing about it. However, we kept preaching to them about Jesus. Finally they asked us to tell them more about him. Then we began a prayer meeting with them. We told them that God only heard the prayers of people who were humble. We knelt with them in a circle, while they held their rifles and bayonets pointed upward. One bandit said he would take Jesus as his Saviour, regardless of the future.

Our new chief also selected Jaffray and Miller to return to Wuchow to raise ransom money.

Our Chinese Christian helper, Ah Tsat, could have gone free and back to his family, but he said, "I feel it is my Christian duty to remain here." He became the go-between for the bandits and the Chinese government officials in making terms for our release.

One dark rainy night I decided to make a break for liberty. But a voice seemed to speak clearly out of the darkness, "No, not tonight. My grace is sufficient for you." So I turned over and slept.

One day all bandits, including the chief, went to meet our boat that had returned from Wuchow with the money on it. It was loaded with armed Chinese soldiers, who said, "We have the money on the boat. Come and get it." The bandits said, "No, you bring it out on the riverbank and we will accept it." The boat just turned and went back down the river.

The bandits returned to our dens in the mountains. That night they were very angry. Ah Tsat listened to their talk and made his report to us in broken English: "Brethren, I—don't think—we—go—back—to—Wuchow,   —I—think—we   go —to—our—heavenly—home." It was a strange hour and a new feeling. The Lord would take care of our families and little ones, we said. "Just a little while now, and we shall be walking in the streets of Paradise with our blessed Lord Jesus." The Lord was so close to us in that testing hour that it was a happy place to be, even though the prospects were that shortly our bullet-ridden bodies would be lying out on the rugged mountainside.

But God still had something for us to do on earth. Eventually, I came to the conclusion that missionary work to the bandits was finished and I should look for God's plan of escape.

In the next camp I received a letter from my wife. It was addressed: "To Rex Ray, with the bandits somewhere in the Kwangsi Mountains." Good mail service! Now I really got homesick and decided to do something about it.

Next day, late in the afternoon as we traveled over the mountains in the pouring rain, I stopped to look things over. In the canyon below us, we could see a little shanty. I was told this was where we would spend the night. I decided I would not. Northward was a wide valley with a river stretching out in the distance. I decided to travel on that river on a log or canoe by night and hide during the day time, until I reached safety somewhere far to the south. I knew this river eventually reached the sea near Hong Kong or Macao.

The problem was how to part company with the guard who was left behind to take me down the mountain, where ten other guards and Brother Carnes had gone to the shanty. I looked my guard over. He wore two belts of cartridges, a dirk knife, and carried a rifle with a bayonet. Tough looker he was! The possibilities were that he might "do" me in instead of my "doing" him in. I prayed, "Lord, you can handle him better than I can. You just put the fear of God in him and make him leave me here alone." Then I began staring at the guard as though I might eat him if he got too close. He began to get nervous; he twisted his hands and walked to and fro. I prayed silently, "Lord, just keep working on him until he makes tracks down the mountain." In a few minutes he started off. When he was about fifty yards away, he raised his rifle and cocked the trigger. I was looking at the shooting end. I could only pray, "Lord, if you don't want him to kill me, just don't let him pull that trigger." The Lord answered, for the bandit started off down the trail.

When he was nearing the shanty, I knew if I started to run, they would all see me, and it would be a long chase back across the mountains. Too, the bandits might take a short cut. I remembered the Lord's promise, "Whatsoever ye shall ask of the Father in my name, he [will] give it you" (John 15:16).

I prayed, "Lord, just send a cloud down over those bandits so they will never know which way I take." Then came floating down beautiful white clouds that passed down into the valley and buried the bandits out of sight. Up where I was, the sun was still shining brightly. "Thank you, Lord." Never before had I appreciated the feeling of freedom as I did at that moment.

Now it was time to put two feet under my prayers. I did that at full speed across and down the mountain. Shortly I rounded an almost perpendicular cliff. I stepped on protruding stones and held onto bunches of grass and small bushes. If one rock had given way or one tuft of grass had loosened, no one would have known what became of Rex Ray. But the Lord promised, "He shall give his angels charge concerning thee . . . lest at any time thou dash thy foot against a stone" (Matt. 4:6).

I left the mountaintop and descended into the canyon below. At times the jungle was so dense that I had to crawl. When I could go no further, I asked the Lord for help. To one side there was a well-worn trail! I traveled on.

Suddenly I came to a village I recognized from the mountain peaks around it. It was headquarters! If I climbed through the brush around the village I would lose much precious time. I was rushing to stay ahead of the news of my escape. I knew the chiefs would send runners into all the mountain gaps and river crossings.

I pushed my heart down again and decided to go right through the village. I knew the Lord could lead me through it as well as around it. I got safely through, but a short distance away, I did what Lot's wife did. I looked back. Lights flashed up all over the village. I guessed correctly that runners had arrived with news of my escape. I started around a little hill, when suddenly right in front of me were a lot of blazing torches, each in the hand of a bandit, I knew. "Lord, save me or these bandits will get me sure," I prayed.

I turned and fled, my feet slipping off the narrow wet path now and then into watery mud. I was determined to rush on, until I was stopped by a bullet or by bandit hands on my throat. On I went until I came to a trail up which the bandits had led us a few nights before. I turned and went up the mountainside on my hands and knees, pulling myself up by muddy grass and bushes, until at last I reached the top. Thank the Lord, those bandits' torches were still at the foot! I felt assured the Lord was going to deliver me completely.

Down the other side of the mountain I sped, sometimes up and sometimes down. I came to a mountain stream of rushing cold water. Through the waistdeep rushing water I waded, drinking a few handfuls of water on the way across. Once I crossed a roaring mountain stream on a footlog, in utter darkness, for overhanging brush shut out all light. About this time I reached into my pocket for a few grains of cooked rice that I had been carrying for weeks. A dried persimmon was the last of my food supply.

Just before dawn I came out on a sand bar, where there was a dark, silent body of water. I bent down a bush for a bed and spread myself out on it on my back. As I lay there, I heard human voices! I could only pray. The men passed by within a few feet of me. They could have heard my thumping heartbeats. As soon as they passed, I quietly arose and followed them, thinking they might lead me out of the jungle. But they didn't go in the direction I wanted to go. (In all of my wanderings I never lost my direction, thanks to the training from my father on the cattle ranges in Indian territory.) On my feet I waited for daylight, when I found a way across the water and a trail along the river.

I passed through a village and on to a riverbank, where I awakened the ferryman, who put me across the river. He was the first man I had seen since I left the bandits the day before. I inquired of the way ahead and speeded up again. I found out later that I had been gone only about thirty minutes when the bandits arrived at the ferry. The Lord knew where I was and where the bandits were, and he kept sufficient distance between us. He led me through all the wild bandit country faster than the bandits could travel their own trails! After I felt a little surer that the bandits would not catch me, I sat down and for the first time poured the sand out of my shoes. My new shoes now had big holes in the bottom, and I could put my socks on from either end, the holes were so big.

I finally reached the bank of the raging Foo River, opposite the walled city of Chiu Ping. I asked some nearby fishermen, who were repairing their nets, to put me across the river to the motorboat anchored on the opposite side, near the city wall.

"Oh, no, the river is too swift," they said. The bandits got all my money except three twenty-cent pieces. One I had used to buy some eggs; another, I had paid the ferryman that morning. Now I had one left. I told the fishermen I would give them all the money I had if they would put me across the river and on that boat.

The fishermen said, "All right, we will do it." They took me a distance up the river, then shot out into the current and down the river and across to the big motorboat. I got out of the canoe and onto the deck of the motorboat. Then I pulled out my pocketbook and opened it up. "There she is, fellows, all the money I've got; one twenty-cent piece!" They were mad enough to throw me back into the river.

The men on the motorboat looked at me dumbfounded. I looked like a third-class hobo. The knees of my pants were out; the buttons on my coat were missing, only strings held it on; my beard was three weeks old, ragged and wild-looking. So I told the boatmen how Jesus had delivered me from the bandits and brought me safely out of the mountain jungles. Then they told me their experience. They had been sent to the city of Chiu Ping by the Chinese government, under orders not to return to Wuchow until they brought one or both of us captives back with them. They had been anchored there for many days, waiting. No wonder their great surprise when suddenly I stood aboard their boat!

The news spread rapidly, and the city officials came to see me. I told them also how Jesus Christ had delivered me out of the hands of the bandits. They were greatly impressed. One replied. "Our gods can't do things like that. Only your God can. I told them to hurry and talk price with the bandits and get Brother Carnes delivered, because he would not try to escape.

The bandits came down on their demands, from the hundred thousand dollars to thirty thousand dollars for Brother Carnes. The officials talked price for another three weeks, with Ah Tsat as go-between. They got the price down to four thousand dollars. Then they arrested several businessmen and put them in jail, telling them that when they put up the four thousand dollars they would be freed. They did that. The money went into the mountains and Brother Carnes was carried out on two bamboo poles, because he was too weak to walk. After he was free, the Chinese government sent soldiers into the bandits' country and captured and shot four hundred of them.

A few weeks after our return to Wuchow, my "police official servant," again well dressed and all smiles, came to my home. He told me that one day, while they were in the hands of the bandits, when Brother Carnes was on his knees praying, he got down and prayed also. Pointing to the New Testament, he said, "This is the most comforting book I ever read." Before captivity, he had had no time to listen to the gospel!

# 3
# Term No. 1 Ended

Communist labor unions put so much pressure on the Chinese Christians early in 1926 that Wuchow was thrown into confusion. The enemies of the gospel took a religious census of the city. Wherever a Christian was found, a placard was nailed over the door saying, "Christians live here." From then on, that home was subject to any persecution the devil's crowd wanted to hurl. A special committee demanded that we hand over all of the mission property—Stout Memorial Hospital, mission residences, and all missionary funds. Then the labor union called a strike against us. All of the Chinese doctors, nurses, and patients were driven out. Under threat of death, Chinese Christians were forced to stay away from the church and our mission compound. Nevertheless, they held their services anyway—in secret!

Mrs. Sin Yee Koo, superintendent of Waang To Girls' School, was arrested. The Reds demanded that she deliver all her girl students to them. She replied, "You can even kill me, but I will never *give* one of the girls to you!" That night the girls were all hidden on the fifth floor of our hospital, then secretly put on boats and sent back into the country to their homes.

Merchants of Wuchow who were our friends were threatened with death if they sold us anything. So there was nothing left to do but nail up our Baptist book store, our residences, the hospital, and everything we had, and leave the city for awhile.

A United States gunboat was anchored in Wuchow. Throughout all one day, we hauled out trunks and everything we could move to the riverbank, where the U. S. Marines stood guard for us. But each trip we made to the riverbank, which was about a quarter of a mile away, howling mobs threw clods at us and shouted every insult they could think of. A Navy officer wanted to attack the mobs, but we told him, "Hold still. We will return some day when the storm is over. If you kill a lot of them, we can never return."

Early the next morning, just when one of the river steamboats was ready to shove off for Canton, the marines and sailor towed our boatload of trunks, boxes, and hospital equipment alongside the steamer and dumped them into it. The Reds rushed to their headquarters to get an order to hold the departing steamer, but before they could get back, Dr. Mansfield Bailey and I were speeding down the river to Canton and Hong Kong.

The Wuchow police were put in charge of the Mission property. The other missionaries boarded the hospital motorboat and were escorted to Canton by the American gunboat.

Mrs. Ray and our children were already on an island near Hong Kong. Within a short time we were on an American ship, sailing to good old U.S.A. and Texas sunshine.

At my boyhood home on the farm west of Bonham, Texas, the children learned to love "Grandma," my mother. After a short time at her home, we purchased a used Model T Ford, loaded it with camping equipment, piled our China family in, and headed north. In Nebraska we visited my brother Claude, then headed east to Chicago to see my brother Dennis and family.

From there we chugged toward Niagara Falls and New York. By this time Ole Man Winter had descended, so Model T slid and rolled southward. The Washington Monument, Richmond, Virginia, and other places in our pathway were left far behind until we rolled into Memphis, Tennessee, at the beginning of the Mississippi flood.

Mrs. Ray and the children went by train to Texas and Grandma's, so Model T and I tackled Arkansas roads, rivers, and washouts. Big cars, little cars, old cars and new, Cadillacs, and my Model T raced through water and mud toward Texas, for it was only three days until Christmas. The water kept getting deeper and deeper. All I could see ahead was muddy water rushing through the brush and trees, although I guessed a highway was somewhere underneath. When Model T was about to swim or become a submarine, I reluctantly decided to *back* out. I didn't dare try turning around. When I got to land again, I turned around and went into town. There I asked a cop about the river I had tried to cross, and he informed me that the water was about fifteen feet deep over the highway. With rain still coming down in torrents, I curled up in the front seat and slept until daylight.

Early next morning, Texas-bound cars—all covered in various shades of Arkansas red mud—headed west toward Oklahoma. After a long hard muddy race, I crossed Red River and was back in Texas.

At home sweet home, with Mother and my wife and kiddies, I joined brothers, sisters, cousins, and all, around that long table loaded with fatted turkey, cranberries, cakes, and pies.

I had planned to do some special study that year in the Seminary at Fort Worth, so we rented a cottage there. But the Foreign Mission Board was in such dire need of funds that I had to continue speaking all over the country in behalf of foreign missions.

March 8, 1928, we boarded the train in Fort Worth, headed for Vancouver, B.C., Canada, on our return journey to China. Just before we reached Vancouver, Mrs. Ray had a relapse of the flu. The ship's doctor immediately put her to bed and I was left in charge of three lively youngsters on various decks of the ship.

Our voyage from Vancouver to Japan was so stormy and rough that we had to stop for days in Japan to repair one of the turbine engines. Finally we continued to Hong Kong, where we boarded the West River steamboat to Wuchow.

# 4
# A Changed China

Back in Wuchow—but with what a difference.

Two years ago our church building was being smashed, the lights were all stolen, the organ broken up, windows broken out. Bolshevik guards stood about the doors lest any should come to worship, the Christians were driven away, and gloom hung over all.

How different now. The same church building was well lighted and the main auditorium filled to capacity. Children were seated all about the rostrum, and the back of the house was jammed with those who were standing. They came to hear the glorious gospel of Jesus Christ. There were more than one hundred who stayed for the inquirers' class after the close of our first preaching service. The people were earnestly seeking salvation.

Evangelistic meetings were begun throughout the city. Night after night for two weeks the multitudes of hungry souls filled our church to capacity. More than two hundred made a profession of faith in Jesus. Our hearts rejoiced in this wonderful change in the attitude of the people toward the message of the cross. (In a letter to the Foreign Mission Board, Published in the September, 1928, *Home and Foreign Fields,* Rex Ray said, "Oh, that our voices could be multiplied into thousands to help rescue these millions who are lost, lost, lost! The Spirit of God is moving the hearts of the heathen. Oh, that he would awaken his children in Christian lands to the crying needs of this great harvest field! If Christian America fails to deliver God's message to the lost of earth, what shall we answer the Master as these poor souls turn away from the gates of glory into outer darkness?

". . . Two missionaries, who have just returned from a seven weeks' preaching journey far back into the highways and hedges, walked more than 350 miles of the way. Everywhere they went the people were anxious to hear about him whose name is Jesus.")

My Uncle Lon Reeves and his sons, Hermon and Russell, of Oklahoma, had given me a fine new tent. The top was divided into three sections and the walls into two parts. These were rolled up and put into large bags. When we began our journeys into the country, these bags—about three hundred pounds each—were carried on long bamboo poles, with a Chinese coolie at each end. Our equipment also included about four hundred folding camp chairs. We looked like a small army, marching along the trails. In other sections of Kwangsi Province we used native oxcarts to haul our equipment.

There was plenty of excitement when we set up the tent on a vacant lot in a village. Great throngs of people came. The tent was usually filled, and sometimes hundreds stood around outside as they listened to the preaching of the gospel. For many it was the first time they had ever heard the name of *Yeso Keituk* (Jesus Christ). Sometimes not one Chinese Christian was there.

I taught the children to sing "Everything's All Right in My Father's House." Later when the children would hear that I was returning they would meet me at the edge of the village, singing, "Everything's All Right in My Father's House." Sometimes we would hear a child in the doorway of his little hut singing, "Yes, Jesus loves me!"

In November, 1930, our little Marian McNair Ray, who was only five years old, was stricken with glandular fever that brought her short, happy life to a close. Doctors did what they could, but the Heavenly Father's call was for her to "come home." Before she left for the hospital and her heavenly journey, she packed her dolls and doll clothes. Later, she said to her mother, "Mommy, I want you to come go with me." Then, as she seemed to catch a view of our mansions in the Father's house, she said, "Mommy, which is our house?" Soon her sweet spirit was carried away by heavenly messengers to await our coming to be with her in the "sweet by and by." Her favorite song that she sang to her little Chinese playmates was "Everything's All Right in My Father's House." We planted her little temple of clay in the Happy Valley Cemetery in Hong Kong.

In Wuchow our boys, David and Dan B., started schoolwork with the Calvert Course, with mother as teacher. Miss Lucille Saunders, daughter of Dr. J. R. Saunders, taught them for a year or so. Later, a Chinese young man taught them until they were ready for our next furlough.

(Editor's Note: The following excerpt from the March, 1928, *Home and Foreign Fields* gives Rex Ray's account of some evangelistic trips.)

Go with me on a missionary journey and see what the Lord is doing. We board a motorboat in Wuchow, . . . then we start upriver. Aboard the boat we have opportunities to give out or sell Christian literature among the passengers, and talk the gospel to them as we journey along the river. We reach the end of our river journey, get our baggage and start inland. We go to our Baptist chapel or preaching hall, if we have one in that city, and when we open the doors and call the people, the men and boys literally pack it full until the preacher looks out upon a mass of yellow faces. Some have heard before, others hear for their first time . . . Some who hear are anxious to learn more about this wonderful Saviour of men. Some accept him as their Saviour, . . . while others reject him. . . .

The next place in which we stop there is no chapel. The people are anxious to hear us preach, so they open up the ancestral hall, in which they have been worshiping their ancestors for ages, and in a short time their hungry hearts are listening to the message of life. On one occasion they were so glad that we visited their village and preached to them that they fired a lot of firecrackers at the close of the service. This is the Chinese way of showing honor.

On a missionary journey back in the mountains . . . a message came from a man far back in the rougher mountains. His message . . . was that when the foreign missionary came along, to send him back into his mountains, as there were several men who wanted to be baptized. . . . I felt the Lord wanted us to go over there and see. So after an all day's hard march through the mountains we arrived at the home of the man who wrote the letter. He invited all the neighbors in to hear the gospel that night. The Chinese preacher and I both preached to a large crowd of men and boys who were seated out under the open sky, while the women and girls stood out to one side in the dark. . . .

The following morning we had an old-fashioned experience meeting, and some of these men told us what great things the Lord had done for them. One by one they told us how they had given up ancestral-worship, devil-worship, gambling, lying, etc., and that now they were following Jesus, were praying to him daily, and they wanted to follow him in baptism.

Both the young Chinese preacher and I were anxious to know how it was that they had found God's plan of salvation away out in those mountains where there had never been a preacher before. [They] told us that their neighbor, Brother Sing, had told them about Jesus. . . . He had gone away to a far city on business and while there he heard the gospel in one of our little chapels. He then and there accepted Jesus as his Saviour, was baptized, and then went back into his mountains to tell his neighbors what . . . the Lord had done for him. As a result of this one lone layman's witnessing, I led eight men and one boy down into the pool and buried them in baptism. . . . It was a testing time for those new Christians. Some of their mothers stood on the bank of the pool and mocked them because these sons had become followers of Jesus.

During the depression, when God's people in the States were hard put for money, the Foreign Mission Board lacked funds to keep the book store in Wuchow open. They ordered it closed, but Janet and I were able for awhile to take enough out of our small salary to keep it open. One morning as I tramped with our army of coolies and the tent equipment, I prayed, "Lord, show me what to do about the book store. If you want it kept open, help me know it. I pray this in Jesus' holy name and for his sake. Amen."

Miles away from Wuchow, we met a man on the trail. When he looked up at this big white man, he said, "Oh, you must be Missionary Rex Ray. I saw you in the book store. I bought a New Testament there and took it home with me and read it. Now I believe in Jesus and I taught my family and they too believe. We have told others who have believed, until there are forty or fifty people who want to be baptized and form a church."

That was the answer to my prayers. If one New Testament in the hands of a heathen Chinese man could win that many souls, it was worth any sacrifice to place Christian literature in the homes. We knew that somehow with God's help we must keep the book store open.

On another trip, we had worked hard until very late, setting up the tent in a village and getting chairs ready for services the next day. We went to bed exhausted. About midnight I was awakened by a Chinese frantically begging me: "My sister is dying. You must come and heal her."

I knew I could not heal the woman. In the first place, I am not even a doctor. But if I did not go and try to help her, we could just as well pull down our tent and move on. So I dressed and went to the tent of our Bible women and asked them to come with me to the house.

The Chinese had already moved the sick woman out of the house to die. If she died in the house, they thought the evil spirits would remain. This would mean that the house would have to be burned.

The only medicine I had with me was some milk of magnesia —in case I got indigestion during the weeks out in the villages. I asked one of the Bible women to boil some water. Then I gave the sick woman some of the warm water and a dose of the medicine. Out loud I prayed, "Lord, you know I have no power to perform miracles. I cannot heal this woman. I have done all I can, and now I leave this woman in your hands. May your will be done."

The woman began to get better immediately. By morning she was able to cook breakfast for her family. Her sickness was a bad case of indigestion—but it was God's way of getting that village ready to receive the missionary.

Not only all kinds of people came to the tent meetings, but also animals. One night before I started to preach, I heard a big commotion. A woman screamed, and a hog squealed. People were getting up and moving quickly toward the edge of the tent. When I turned around I saw a Chinese woman sitting in a chair being carried about on the back of a frightened hog. The animal had wandered into the tent and somehow wriggled under the woman's chair. Now he was twisting and turning and streaking about the tent, trying to get loose from his prison. He really broke up the meeting until we rescued the woman and got the chair off his back!

During the winter of 1931–32, our evangelistic tent was spread in four different cities in Kwangsi Province. Our party included two colporteurs, two Chinese evangelists, and myself. Thousands of people heard the message of salvation, many of them for the first time. The Chinese people listened to the preaching of God's Word as never before. Many turned away from the ways of darkness and idolatry to follow Jesus.

Two nights before I was to preach in a big new chapel in a new town, bandits raided the place. So during our night preaching services soldiers were stationed about the front doors to prevent a raid upon our people. Some officials sat in the audience with their own rifles in their hands. Night after night the chapel was packed full of earnest listeners to the preaching of the gospel, and a number accepted Christ as Saviour and Lord.

A group of young evangelists from North China came to Wuchow. They preached Christ and him crucified as the only remedy for sin and the hope of salvation. Hundreds of luke-warm Christians got right with God and then went out after the lost. There was praying and rejoicing, the like of which I had never seen in China before. The evangelist who did most of the preaching got his Ph.D. degree from an American university. While studying at Union Theological Seminary, he had attended a Baptist church in New York and was gloriously converted. He was immediately pronounced crazy and sent to an insane asylum, from which his Chinese consul rescued him three days later. Now here he was, literally wearing himself out physically in his eagerness to bring his people to Jesus.

Late one afternoon near the northeast corner of the city wall of Nanning, where Dr. P. H. Anderson and I were conducting a revival, I knelt in prayer. I began to feel like Jacob wrestling with the angel at Peniel. The longer I wrestled in prayer, the more I felt that I could not let go until the Lord flooded my very soul with his presence and power. Then heaven did seem to come down and surround me, until my very heart was melted with tears and I knew what it meant really to be filled with the Spirit. When the hour came for that night's service, I felt that it was not I but the Lord preaching through me. In all my life I had never felt such power. Truly life has never been the same for me since that wonderful sunset experience.

The Lord thus prepared me for another hour I was soon to face at San Hui. News came that an endurance struggle against wrong was drawing near a close. For fourteen long, heartbreaking years, Mrs. Ray and I had tried to patiently endure, for Jesus' sake, opposition to our work by one who was supposed to be our friend. Alone with the Lord on the bank of a mountain stream, I received assurance that our long-suffering in this matter would soon end. Back in my study in Wuchow, after the opposing one had left China—seemingly as a martyr—a great burden came into my heart to pray that he would break down before he reached America and confess his sins. The Lord assured me this prayer would be answered, and peace came into my soul.

When the man reached Rome, he did break down and confess his sins to his wife. He wrote a letter to our mission, admitting he was guilty of all the charges made against him. He enclosed a check for five hundred dollars to make restitution to the Chinese whom he had wronged financially. He also wrote me a personal letter, asking forgiveness for the wrongs he had done me and the evil he had wished against me those fourteen years. I wrote him the most Christian letter that I knew how to write. I told him I hoped we could join hands and walk as brothers in Christ until time for us to cross over to life's other side.

After another seven years, things were shaping up for us to return to America on furlough. Before we took off, Dr. Charles E. Maddry, secretary of the Foreign Mission Board, Mrs. Maddry, and Dr. and Mrs. Weatherspoon arrived in China for an inspection tour.

John Lake chartered a ship at Hong Kong that week in 1935 and took us—the Maddrys, Weatherspoons, and a large group of Chinese Baptists—to visit Tai Kam Island Leper Colony. It was a happy hour when Dr. Maddry and others brought greetings to the Tai Kam Baptist Church, composed of 135 lepers. Dr. and Mrs. Lake became members of that lonely island church. And it was he who led in building enlarged facilities to house other hundreds of lepers.

# 5
# Seeing America and Japan

At furlough time, in 1935, a large Norwegian freighter lay at anchor in Hong Kong. It was much cheaper to travel on a freighter than on a passenger ship, so we got aboard. The ship only carried eight passengers, and we accounted for six. Two new members had been added to our little family during our last sojourn in China: Lois Ellen, who was now six, and Mary Dee, who was two.

The ship's Chinese cook started out by serving us corned beef and cabbage; then he served cabbage and corned beef for the next meal. After a few days of this, Mrs. Ray descended into the galley. The meals were delightful during the rest of the voyage.

Just before sunrise one morning, my little daughter Lois bounced out on deck as she shouted at the top of her voice, "Papa, I see America! Papa, I see America!"

We landed happily at Long Beach, California, where we got the new Ford V-8 car that was awaiting our arrival. It was now more than seven years since we had sorrowfully parted company with our faithful Model T.

Seated in the new Ford, with a folding camp trailer following us, we headed across the mountains and deserts of southern California, the blazing sands of Arizona and New Mexico to the plains of western Texas. What a shouting time it was when we rolled up to Mother's little home at Black, Texas. Mother welcomed us at the front gate with outstretched arms. I think it will be much the same when we enter our heavenly home.

We rented a little cottage in Amarillo, Texas, where David and Dan B. entered junior high school. Since they were already world travelers, they were called upon to make speeches on their experiences before the whole school. Lois entered her first American school and eagerly set to work learning American ways.

When we leave the mission field, we say, "When I get home, I'll rest." Now I am putting it this way, "When I get across that last great river at the end of life's journey, I'll sit down on the bank of the river and rest under the shade of the trees."

I hurried across several states to attend the Southern Baptist Convention. I traveled in many states, speaking and showing films which I had taken in China.

Christmas time in 1935 began the last Ray roundup at Mother's little home in the West. My five brothers—Claude, Don, Hez, Dave, and Dennis—and one sister, Price (sister Lynn in California could not attend ) arrived safely with their families. Fortunately, there was a schoolhouse nearby where we parked all the men and boys for the nights. It was a glorious, happy time for all of us, although somehow we knew it was to be our last Christmas together at Grandma's.

The following August, our little family again packed into our Ford and trailer, visited my mother for our last good-bye, and resumed our journey to China. Mother would never really say good-bye. Just after we started off, we remembered something left behind. Mrs. Ray went back to get it and found

Mother in her closet weeping and saying, "I'll never see my boy Rex and his family again on earth."

We drove across northwest Texas and northeast New Mexico with wet towels on top of our heads because of the terrible heat, thence into Colorado, and on to the great Northwest.

In Seattle we loaded our earthly possessions aboard a Japanese passenger ship. A small, undated folder, issued by the shipping company, fell into my hands. It was an appeal for Americans to visit Japan, bringing their own cars with them. Nearing Japan, I requested the purser to set our car on the wharf when we docked.

Our ship was due to stay in Yokohama for a week. So I took my little folder to the shipping company's office and told the officials, "Here we are. We brought our car with us, and now we are ready to see Japan in our car, according to this folder and this request." They tried to get out of the deal, but I refused to take no for an answer. I told them they were an honorable company and I expected them to carry out their promises.

They sent one of their men to make arrangements with customs for me to bring my car ashore. That took all of one day. We still had to run many hurdles, including five sets of police officers and test grounds for drivers—my American driver's license meant nothing to them.

Having bade good-bye to my official helper, I sped up the street to a filling station, tanked up, got a complete road guide for all the roads of Japan, and drove back to our ship, where Mrs. Ray and the children were waiting.

After supper we loaded the children into the car and hit Japan's highways. Through a lot of navy yards, we went on and on. Far in the night we turned back toward Yokohama. We got back into the city but could not find our ship. Not knowing one word of Japanese, we were until after midnight finding it.

Next morning our cabin boy fixed lunches enough to last us all day, and we were ready to venture forth again.

Our first stop was at Kamakura, the site of the very large statue of Buddha. We made pictures, then entered the side door in the idol and climbed the winding stairway up into the head. It was pathetic to see people there, burning incense on altars. Also at Kamakura, we drove onto the famous black sand beaches for a plunge into the surf.

The farther south we went, the poorer the highways grew. Roads were filled with Japanese bicycles, pulling little two-wheeled trailers. Our car horn made no impression on them. They just kept pedaling their bikes in the middle of the road. When we met buses or trucks in towns, we had to drive out to one side, creep along under store awnings, or just stop until the other vehicle passed. Added to this, I had to conform to the Japanese rule of driving on the left side of the road. By sunset, we had reached the heights of the mountains in the Myonoshto area, where we could view in the far distance Japan's great Mount Fuji.

We stayed at the beautiful resort hotel in the high, cool mountain air until after midnight, so we might have the open highways for the return to Yokohama. The children here saw roosters with tail feathers twelve feet long.

With the children sound asleep in the family bus, we zig-zagged and hairpinned down from the heights of that lonely mountain. Once again out on the highway, we drew long breaths of relief and headed back toward our ship in Yokohama. Suddenly coming toward us were bright headlights, glaring right into our faces! It was the Japanese army on the move. Trucks, trucks, and trucks—in full war paint! The drivers were all telling us to stop, surrender, or commit hari-kari. The louder they yelled, the faster I drove. A Japanese officer in a little doodlebug car stopped just in front of us. We stopped. He got out and rushed over to us, sputtering in Japanese and at the same time motioning for us to turn around and head back whence we had come. I kept pointing ahead and yelling, "Yokohama—Yokohama—Yokohama—!" He kept yelling and pointing in the other direction. Another car came up behind him. He went over to this car and finally motioned for us to proceed in the direction we wanted to go. We were relieved when we drove along the wharf beside our ship. With moving pictures of the children playing on the black sand beaches of Japan, in the rolling waves of the ocean, and with other still pictures stored in our film boxes, we were ready for new adventures in Kobe, our next port.

Since Kobe was the end of the voyage for our ship, we were to stay in a hotel there until the company had another ship ready to proceed to Hong Kong. Since we were traveling on tourist-class tickets, some other missionaries told us that we would be placed in a second-class Japanese hotel in Kobe. I replied that I was going to ask for the Tor Hotel, French operated, the finest in the city. As our ship docked in Kobe, a red-headed Frenchman met us on the first-class deck. I wore my finest blue serge suit and my ten-gallon cowboy hat, and Mrs. Ray and the children were in their best clothes. I told the Frenchman, who was representing the great Tor Hotel, that my family and I would like to stop with them for a week at the shipping company's expense. He said he would speak to the shipping company's manager who would come aboard soon.

Shortly, an important-looking little fellow came hopping up the gangplank. Frenchy told him something about us in Japanese. I don't know whether Frenchy said that we owned half of Texas, or just two fifths of it. Mr. Manager took one look at us, and everything was "O.K., O.K., very O.K." Our personal baggage was hustled off the ship and headed through the very particular customs.

One important little official was very anxious to get his nimble fingers into every crevice and corner of our bags. The cork had come out of a bottle which contained honey and almond cream, and the cream had spread out into the clothes. This official thrust his fingers deep into the cream. When he jerked his hand out of the bag and beheld the slimy stuff clinging to his hand, his expression changed to that of horror at the pollution and defilement. (We did not laugh there, but later!) The examination of our baggage suddenly ended.

At the Tor Hotel we were installed in the finest rooms, with fluffy beds and all the trimmings for our whole family. When we appeared in the dining halls, there were daintily dressed Japanese maids to give the children the finest foods that Japan could produce. It was one week of enjoying the good things without a worry.

However, as we read the Japanese daily papers, we could clearly see the rising of war clouds. Japan was getting ready to attack China. We were really anxious to get out of Japan and back to our work.

# 6
# Blockade Runner

In Shanghai we transferred David and Daniel B. to a steamboat going up the Yangtze River. Far up the river, they went ashore and up the mountains to Kuling to attend an American school. We proceeded to Hong Kong and then to Wuchow, then on to where we unloaded our Ford V-8 for a new kind of travel for us in China. Formerly, I had traveled by Chinese passage boats and then walked many miles overland and down the mountains. Now, automobile roads had been built so we could carry the gospel to many new places in Kwangsi.

I fitted out our car and baggage trailer for a long country trip, on which also went our veteran missionary, Miss Mollie McMinn, on her *last* missionary journey. We also had with us a new missionary, Miss Jessie Green, from Georgia, on her *first* trip, Miss Miriam Taoi, and a boy cook.

The Japanese attacked China in the summer of 1937, and war was on. Many factions of Chinese armies who had been fighting each other quickly united against their common enemy. Soon Japanese planes began to bomb Wuchow. There were no adequate air raid shelters in Wuchow, so great throngs

49

of people rushed to Stout Memorial Baptist Hospital for shelter. The hospital was a five-story brick, steel, and concrete building, the safest in Wuchow.

During the first big raid, Mrs. Ray and I took our two little girls (Lois, about seven, and Mary Dee, three) to the hospital for refuge also. We felt that Lois, being older, would understand and not be frightened and that Mary Dee would be terribly frightened. When the Jap bombers began power-diving and dropping their deadly bombs, the effect was just the reverse: Lois threw her arms about her mother's neck, screaming and praying. Mary Dee contentedly munched on her red apple. Knowing that the war might go for years, I took Mrs. Ray and our girls for safety to a little cottage on Cheung Chow Island near Hong Kong. Then I returned to Wuchow.

Japan threw a blockade around the entire seacoast of the country, thus cutting off all supplies of medicine and other essentials. Knowing that our hospital could not carry on without supplies, I decided to run the Japanese blockade—a very dangerous operation.

About a hundred miles downriver from Wuchow, I left the riverboat and went ashore near Shiuhing to catch a bus overland to the South. As we waited for a bus, Jap planes attacked us with bombs and machine guns. Waiting passengers and soldiers scattered in every direction for hiding places. I jumped into a nearby drain ditch and stretched out lengthwise, trying to hide under a big bunch of grass overhanging the bank. Never had I liked the idea of someone finding Rex Ray with a lot of bullet holes in his back, so I lay there, face up. The planes looked like big, red-eyed devils roaring toward me, saying "Oh, we'll get you this time!" Then they would zoom right over me, back up into the air, circle and power-dive from the other direction right at me, still spraying their lethal pellets. They kept on and on until I thought they would never stop. I kept making promises to the Lord if he would save me from this threatening death. I could hear an officer under some bamboo bushes nearby telling his Chinese soldiers, "Don't move, don't move." Just then a plane turned and came right up my ditch, sputtering death. I thought, "This is where I get it—bullet holes from feet to head!" But it didn't get me! Then the planes left.

There was one bus there, and when the big fat driver returned, he jumped into his bus and took off at top speed. Not a passenger had an opportunity to get on board. When another bus finally arrived many people rushed into it like prairie dogs running into their hole in the ground. When no one else could get inside, others began climbing up the sides of the bus. They poked their feet inside through the windows and then thrust in their heads, with the rest of their bodies hanging outside. Off waddled the bus, twice overloaded. I decided to chance death at the hands of Jap gunners, rather than suffocate in that bus. At last others of us chartered another bus. Near sundown we reached a town, where we hired a private car to rush us to a place where we caught a big Chinese passage towboat. Just after daylight we debarked and boarded sampans heading up a long canal through the flat rice country toward Macao, a Portuguese city. The day before, Jap planes had machine-gunned many people to death in that area. We anxiously tried to get away before more planes came. Far up the canal, a big junk loaded with brick had grounded crosswise in the canal, so the many boats behind it, with their hundreds of excited, frightened passengers, could not move. Two other passengers in my boat and I left our boat and hit the trail along the banks of the canal. Past the stranded boat, we hired a small boat and at sunrise started rowing frantically up the canal toward our much desired haven of Macao. Grabbing an oar, I showed them how well a missionary could row. All day long we kept those oars biting the muddy waters in the canals, creeks, and rivers, always scanning the horizon for a glimpse of approaching enemy killers. After many long hours of backbreaking rowing under a scorching sun, our little sampan brought us nearer safety. How comforting to see the sun go down! Not only was it cooler, but the Japs could not find us. On we rowed until we caught sight of twinkling lights along the shore at Macao. The lights of heaven could hardly cheer my soul much more than did the lights of Macao at the end of that frightful day's journey! In Macao I boarded a ship to Hong Kong and then a ferry out to Cheung Chow where my family awaited my coming. Happy reunion!

In Hong Kong word got around that I was preparing to run the Jap blockade back into China. I was beseiged by requests from people wanting to go with me. I told them all that I could not guarantee the safety of anyone, not even of myself or my cargo. The party that I collected was composed of twelve Chinese ladies—teachers and students—a Chinese pastor and his family, two German doctors who had escaped Hitler, one British Red Cross nurse and a big fat American who had come to China especially to get experience to write a book. He got it!

We loaded all our cargo and baggage on two Chinese junks in Macao. Then, in a gentle breeze, we sailed out through the harbor toward the setting sun.

Between Macao and the mainland of China we had to cross the open sea. There were two great dangers confronting us— being run down by the Japanese Navy if we tried to cross in the daytime and Chinese pirates if we tried to make the run at night. We chose to risk the pirates.

About dark a long, narrow boat, filled with silent men using paddles, headed straight toward us. They were collecting "protection fees," they informed us. We paid, no questions asked! (We never learned where their protection began or ended.)

On we sailed. Then we spied more silent men in another long boat, with paddles dipping gently into the sea, and two more shooting irons. Knowing they could spit bullets and fire right into your face with a slight touch on their triggers makes your high blood pressure show no sign of dropping, even though your knees may feel like doing so! We paid and sailed on over the moonlit sea for another two hours.

More silent men paddling in a long boat, with their chief in the bow, trying to look down the barrels of two very big guns at the same time. They were different! They only wanted five hundred dollars Hong Kong currency quick! or quicker! I tried to reason with the spokesman, stating that we had already paid. He told me; "Do you see those lights yonder on those islands? If you don't pay up at once I'll take you, your boats, and your whole party over there. Four hundred of our family are waiting over there!" "Oh, sure, Mister, we'll pay you right away. Wait until I take up a collection for you," I said. I turned to our party. "Folks, as you see, we need five hundred dollars right quick!" It was the fastest collection I ever took—Chinese, Germans, Americans, and British all dug for cold cash. Again we paid and sailed on. We did not need any fans to cool us off, but we did need mop rags to wipe the cold sweat from our aging brows.

Two hours later more silent paddlers glided toward us. This time one of the German doctors was ready to put up a fight, but I was in charge, so we paid again and sailed on for another two hours. The next bunch was different—they swarmed onto our boats, which had been lashed together, and began taking what they could find. When they discovered that some of the girls had rolled greenbacks up in their hair, they began grabbing gals, hair-dos, money, and all. One spunky little teacher had her fists doubled up, with fire blazing from her eyes. Just as I went over to help her, a long, lanky pirate poked his young cannon into my ribs and yelled at me to get back on the other boat. Finally, with our party (if not our funds) still intact, we sailed on.

About sunrise we reached an island occupied by Chinese troops. What a sigh of relief from all of us! But we still had to cross one big river patrolled by Japanese Navy boats. I had lost all of my money but not my valuable cargo of drugs nor Dr. Beddoe's baggage that I had with me. (Dr. Beddoe, having just returned from America, had decided to go by plane to Wuchow.)

We decided to hire long canal boats from Chinese farmers. We covered the drugs and baggage with rice straw and sent the boats across the river to the mainland of China, with a prayer for the boatman and the cargo.

Then we waited until after midnight to push our boats out into the moonlit river. Success or failure would be decided within an hour. We sailed up and across the mile-wide river and entered the mouth of the canal on the mainland, when lo, out of the shadows soldiers cried out, "Halt! Who are you?" (They were traitor-soldiers, working for the Japanese.) They said, "Drop anchor until sunrise." The girls feared that these traitors might turn them over to the Japs. They knew it would be better to have their throats cut and be thrown into the river than to fall into the hands of roving Jap soldiers.

When day came, I persuaded the Cantonese leader to let us go on our way, since we had neither money nor goods. (He did not know we had sent boatloads on ahead.) Seeing there was no chance for profit, their leader finally told us to go on. Through the canal we traveled. About 11:00 A.M. we came to a village, and there, along the banks, our cargo boats were waiting! We loaded our baggage and medical supplies back into our junks and traveled inland. When we heard Japanese planes coming, we hid our boats along the banks, and everybody ducked for cover.

After much anxious travel, we came to the end of our water-

ways and unloaded passengers and cargo at a town w...
Chinese soldiers were stationed. Learning of our mission, the
commanding officer put on a big feast in our honor, and the
next day he drafted about one hundred people to carry our
goods overland to a place where we could get steamers to
Wuchow.

Aboard a big riverboat for Wuchow, we felt our anxieties
fading away. At Shiuhing, the young ladies went ashore,
being near their homes. Another day, and we landed safely
at Wuchow without a loss of cargo or people. It was a happy
hour for me when I saw those medical supplies passing
through the gates and into the hospital.

# 7
# Bombs and More Blockades

A year or so later, on my way downriver to Hong Kong, I boarded a Chinese towboat. Jessie Green and two other Christian ladies were also on board. Just before the boat was to sail, an air raid alarm was sounded. There was no time to reach the air raid tunnels under the mountains back of the hospital. Nothing could we do but wait and pray. Eighteen Jap bombers roared up and down the river and over the city. As bombs exploded all about us, everything in our boat began crashing and smashing. The sides of the boat were coming in, the roof down, the decks up. Broken glass and splintered wood flew in all directions. A mighty giant seemed to be smashing us to pieces. People on all sides were dying. After the last bomb had exploded and the planes had roared away, I decided to get up and look. From the rear windows of the boat, I saw nine more planes coming up the river wing tip to wing tip. I needed no invitation to return and join the prayer meeting where the three Christian ladies were on their faces calling on the Lord for mercy. I fell on my hands and knees and placed a duffel bag on top of my head, hoping it would stop the bomb fragments. I could only pray,

"Lord, if you have any more work for me to do on earth, please don't let these bombs destroy me."

The next few seconds were the most nerve-testing that I have ever experienced. We could hear the bombs whistling through the air directly toward us, as we braced ourselves, expecting any second to be blown into fragments. Then it was over! I opened my eyes. My face was eight or ten inches from the deck, and under my face was the back of a Chinese woman's head. She had faith in our praying and had stuck her head under mine for safety. Her faith was justified—she didn't get a scratch!

As the planes roared away, I arose and went outside to look again. Everything was on fire—the city and all the boats and buildings along the shore. The big floating pier was a roaring mass of flames. All about us, boats were sinking and burning; fragments of human beings were scattered everywhere. Great throngs of people drowned in the flooding waters of the river. All the gangways leading from the piers to the shore had been blown away. Our own boat would be a roaring inferno within minutes. "Hurry out!" I yelled to Miss Green, Miss Tsoi, and the other Christian woman, none of whom had been hurt. While they were coming, I grabbed my new motorcycle and threw it into the river, hoping that fishermen could find it for me later.

Two of the ladies could swim a little; the other could not. Downriver was a floating pier not yet on fire. Big anchor chains held it in place. With this as our goal, I jumped into the river, and Miss Tsoi followed me. When she came to the surface, she grabbed at me, tearing the front of my shirt to shreds before I could tow her to the anchor chain downstream. I towed Miss Green to the chain also. The other Chinese woman then jumped in. When she came up, all I could see were two little kicking feet. I grabbed and brought her face out of the water. The swift river was carrying us downstream.

I thrust out my right hand and caught the last anchor chain on the lower side of the last pier, pulling the almost drowned woman to it.

I swam shoreward but was so nearly exhausted it seemed I would drown. When I remembered how to float, inhaling all the air possible, I went floating down the river like an inflated frog. I drifted beside a little boat in which a man was standing, rowing upstream. Two girls in the boat were screaming because they thought I would capsize their sampan and drown them. I only clutched the side of the boat, however, and they dragged me toward the south bank of the river. They let me off onto the big rudder of a junk, where I perched until rescued by a customs motor launch. We rushed back across the river to the burning city, but there was no sign of life near the big floating pier where I had last seen Miss Tsoi. The pier itself was a roaring mountain of fire. Our Chinese boat, on which were our baggage, movie camera, and money, had already been devoured by the flames.

The motor launch headed down the river and picked up Miss Green and the other little woman. After we were put ashore, I led Miss Green along by the hand, both of us barefooted. She pleaded, "Please, Mr. Ray, won't you borrow that Chinese man's coat for me?" (She had lost her outer clothing in the river.) I replied, "Come on, Sis, these people are not watching you. They see only the fires, death, and destruction."

When we reached the Baptist Mission compound, our beloved Dr. William Wallace met us just inside the hospital gates. "Parson," he said, "they hit us pretty hard today." (He always called me "Parson.") His operating clothes were bloody from his chin to his feet.

We returned to the riverfront in search of Miss Tsoi. About two weeks earlier, she had undergone major surgery and we thought she surely must have succumbed. But we found her

alive and well, under the care of a Christian Chin
from our Baptist Mission in Canton. Truly the Lo.
for his own!

Great gaping holes had been blasted through the concrete
and steel roof of the fifth floor of Stout Memorial Hospital.
Doors had been blown off the hinges; shattered window glass
was showered all over the floors; rubbish, broken plaster, and
dirt littered the whole hospital. Bruised, broken, torn, bleeding bodies of men, women, and children were everywhere.
Every bed held a victim, up and down the corridors on every
floor lay suffering people of all ages and sizes, helpless, groaning, bleeding—and many dying. Inside the operating room, Dr.
Wallace, with his faithful nurses and doctors, was operating,
patching, bandaging, soothing, and administering to the suffering as rapidly as possible. The whole place looked more
like a slaughterhouse than a hospital. Across the way, Waang
To Girls' School was burning. The crying needs were more
than we could meet.

As I went up and down the halls among this mass of
butchered humanity, loved ones begged me to use *ta cham*
(the needle) to ease the suffering. I could only reply that
the doctors and nurses were working as fast as they could.
I shall never forget one little girl, lying there on the cold concrete floor. A slug had torn her innocent little face; the color
was fading from her cheeks as life ebbed away in a little
red rivulet winding across the floor.

Along in the night I went down in the basement to visit
the *peng-on-fong* (room-of-peace). All was silent. Death was
sitting there grinning at me! Yes, he had had the last say.
There were thirty-eight men, women, and children there.

Once more I headed south, down the great West River toward Hong Kong. Far below Shiuhing, I hit the delta country
and caught a little motor launch to San Ooi. A Chinese
man on his way to Macao was on the boat. I had two travel

boxes of baggage; he had no baggage at all. When we left the boat, he piloted me across miles of flat rice country to the outskirts of San Ooi. He pointed out the Japanese outposts and led through crooked alleys and back streets into the city. On a side street we entered a Chinese shop. My new friend hired a coolie to carry my baggage. He told me that just around the corner was a barbed wire barricade and Japanese guard. I dressed in khaki. My friend wanted me to change to civilian clothes, but I refused. I told him that if I got picked up by the Japanese, he was not to let on that he had ever seen me, because I did not want him to get into trouble. Sure enough, there stood the Japanese sentry. My baggage coolie was just ahead of me. I gave the sentry a quick military salute. Instead of challenging me, he jumped to attention, his rifle frozen upright in front of him. I thought, "Boy, you stay frozen until I get through this barbed wire and everything will be just fine." He did!

Inside the barricade, Jap guards were playing cards or something with the Chinese interpreter. I gave a snappy salute and marched on, looking neither to the right nor to the left. The Chinese interpreter laughed and said in English, "Very good, very good." I thought, Yes, it is very good if you fellows will sit right where you are and let me march on. They did—and I did.

Around the corner at the bus station I changed my Chinese money into Japanese, boarded the bus, and took off for Kong Moon. A curious little Jap soldier on the bus wanted to find out who I was. I told him in English that I was an American. He didn't get it. Then I told him in Chinese, and still he didn't get it. Finally, I asked one of the passengers to write for him in Chinese that I was an American. His face lit up with a big smile as he hopped around repeating, "Melican, Melican, Melican." I was glad he seemed friendly.

We came to an iron bridge. All the passengers were ordered

out to cross the bridge ahead of the bus. Chinese policemen and Jap soldiers searched the passengers, but I just walked around them. The bus came across, and the Jap friend began explaining, "Camerah, Camerah, Camerah," but soon shoved the guard aside, closed the lids of my boxes, and announced the "all clear" to the bus driver. The Chinese passengers piled back into the bus and we were off again in a happy mood. I was especially relieved, because in war times, a Japanese sees red at the word "camera." It is as dangerous as showing a GI a live grenade with your fingers on the firing pin.

Once in the streets of Kong Moon, we began hunting a room in a hotel. We had run the gauntlet safely and never once had been challenged or asked for identity or passport. No more guards now. My Chinese friend had kept a watchful eye on me from a distance. Now he found it convenient to stop in the same hotel I did. Early next morning he came and whispered to me that a stoppage of all boats leaving Kong Moon had been ordered by the military. The place was full of American-Chinese who were struggling to get out of China. My Chinese friend showed me where he carried his Hong Kong money inside a slit in his jacket collar. All he had in his pockets or pinned on his jacket were Japanese passes. He could come and go anywhere he wished without hindrance and seemed to know everything the Japs were doing.

I decided to go to Japanese military headquarters and bum a ride on an airplane or on a military boat to Macao. They brought out their stenographer and hauled me on the carpet for a thorough military quiz. They wanted to know where from, my name, why in their town, how I got through the Chinese front lines. That one was easy. When the Chinese saw I was American, they had said, "Friend, pass on."

The Jap wise ones never asked me how I got through their lines. They wanted information about the Chinese, but I had none to give. Then they found in my pocket a copy of a receipt I had given their Japanese consul in Hong Kong the year before, and their eyes popped out. Their Jap consul had paid me seven hundred dollars Hong Kong currency, after the Jap airmen had bombed us into the river and burned my baggage and camera. I had gone in person to present a bill for my losses. The Jap consul had replied, "We don't do things that way."

"You want America to remain your friend? If you don't pay me for my losses, I'm certainly going to talk." I acted as though all America would jump to help me if he didn't pay me at once.

He thought a bit, then said, "You wait here." In a little while he returned with the seven hundred dollars and asked for a receipt. I gladly wrote him one, but kept an exact copy of it lest there should be rumors later.

With excitement rising, my interrogators asked me, "What is the meaning of this receipt?" The Bible tells us that when we are brought before rulers, the Holy Spirit will give us the words to speak. I replied, "Gentlemen, that is a very private affair between the Honorable Japanese Consul and me. Therefore I cannot tell you anything about it." Up to that time, they suspected that I was a spy for China or for America. Now they didn't know what to think. Since their own government had paid me all that money, I might be a spy working for Japan. They decided to keep me until they could consult with their own government. They took me to the finest Chinese hotel, engaged a suite of rooms for me, and told the manager of the hotel to charge the bill to the Japanese government. I was forbidden to visit certain parts of the city, then I was left alone.

After a few days I decided to see how closely they were watching me. I rented a bicycle from a Chinese and rode off in the direction of the missionaries' home, five miles away. No one stopped me. When I came to a bridge guarded by

Chinese policemen and Japanese soldiers, I gave the guards a snappy salute, looked eagerly ahead as though I were boss of the show, and rode on.

At the Canadian Mission hospital, the missionaries were amazed. They had not known I was near. Besides, they and the nearby Catholic bishop were not allowed to leave their houses. After tea and a friendly visit, I said, "I had better be on my way back to the hotel. My friends might get worried about me. What if they have changed guards at the bridge and I cannot get back into the city?" I decided to try to return as boldly as I had left. At the bridge, sure enough, new guards were there. Another snappy salute, however, and I rode uneasily past the unsuspecting sentinels, back to my "hotel" prison.

I secretly sent runners to the American consuls in Hong Kong and Canton. When the American consul in Canton learned that I was being held prisoner by the Japanese in Kong Moon, he began eating up the Jap consul by chunks. "The idea of holding an American as a prisoner and not telling us about it!" The Jap gendarme chief came secretly before day in his private car and put me on the fastest boat for Canton. Upon our arrival, the officers rushed ashore, leaving me alone on the boat. Feeling peeved, I hunted up the Japanese captain of the boat and told him that since they had taken me as their prisoner, they should escort me to my own consul. I was put on an American warship and sent to Hong Kong. Thus ended my visit with the Japanese invaders of China. Praise the Lord! He delivered me safely. Many prayers were answered.

In December, 1940, I arrived in Hong Kong from Wuchow, and went at once to the American President Steamship Lines and booked passage for Mrs. Ray and our four children to sail home early in January, 1941. Our two boys had escaped out of the war zone at Kuling, far up in the mountains of China. Since that time they had attended the British school in Kowloon and more recently an American school on Cheung Chow Island, where Lois, eleven, was also a student.

When Mrs. Ray learned that I had booked passages for them to sail, she wanted to wait until my regular furlough time.

"No!" I insisted. "War is going to break out between Japan and the States. I don't know how soon, but when it does, I want you and the children safely in Texas. I will try to dodge the bombs for myself, but I could never dodge them for all of you."

On the appointed day I bade them good-bye and saw the water widen between us as they sailed away. At the last minute, the American school decided to leave on the same boat. What a merry trip they had, carrying on classes under crowded refugee conditions! There was sadness too, however, for never again would many of them see the land of their birth.

I locked up our little cottage on Cheung Chow Island. I felt that it would never be our home again. Then I walked down the winding paths to the ferry to Hong Kong, where I had purchased the last lot of food and medical supplies that I would ever try to run through a Japanese blockade. When all of my supplies were safely loaded, I went to the cabin my ticket called for. Behold, the ticket office had sold the other bunk in the cabin to a customs officer's wife who lived in Wuchow. I called the purser and demanded another cabin. He said I could travel in the dining saloon on the upper deck. Three Japanese army officers had parked themselves in that room.

These snoopy officers eyed my two hundred packages or more of medical supplies and food. There was no denying they were mine, because my name was plainly written on all of them. The Japs had no authority to interfere while on the high seas, but I had no idea what their plans were after we got to Fort Byaird. Deliberately, I did not list my cargo on the ship's manifest, so I could be free to unload my goods the instant we docked. Aboard ship was an experienced blockade runner, whom I hired to help me. He was among the first ashore. Immediately he hired two big junks and a bunch of coolies for me. The coolies boarded the ship and began throwing my cargo over the side into the junks, working as though the ship were on fire. As the junks touched shore, the coolies ran with my stuff to a storage place. Shortly, my assistant arrived with a big truck and we stacked it high with the balance of my cargo. As soon as the last bundle was on the truck we drove away at full speed to a garage inside the high compound wall at the Baptist Mission. The doors were quickly locked and everyone leisurely departed as though we knew nothing.

After dark, the part of the cargo that had been hidden in the city was moved to our compound. Just after daylight, the cargo truck moved out on the highway, followed by a station wagon carrying our Chinese lady doctor and others. When guards stopped us, I told them to talk to the driver of the station wagon. When they went back to talk to him, I told my truck driver to step on the gas. Since the guards were on foot, we escaped toward the border town eight miles away. Once there, we quickly unloaded everything into a mission chapel and closed the doors. That evening, I engaged a coolie boss to supply me with enough coolies to carry my whole shipment across country on a three-day trip.

That night I went for a walk in Kwong Chau Waan, right on the border between French territory and China. Whom should I meet but my Japanese ex-cabinmates! They wanted to know if I planned to try entering China. I told them that perhaps some day I would try it.

About daylight the next morning, with my coolie train equipped, shod, loaded, and ready to march, I gave the word and off they went in single file. No use trying the highway. It was blocked with barbed wire and guards. But our coolie boss knew a secret passage across a foot-wide stone bridge. Once across that bridge, we would be in China and safe. I followed the train on my bicycle. When the last coolie crossed the China end of that bridge, my heart poured out grateful thanks and praise to the Heavenly Father for his guidance and protection of my precious cargo of medical supplies.

For four days our burdened coolies slowly wound their way across hills and plains, through rain and red mud. Several times we had to hide from Japanese machine-gunning planes. Near Wat Lam, I went ahead of the carriers, riding my bicycle. Inside the city gate, I started for the church, where I hoped to find water to drink. Before I had gone very far, there came an air raid. People ran in every direction. One stream of fleeing people made for open country, and so did I. I reached some bamboo bushes about half a mile from town and dived under. The Japs strafed the town, then flew right over my head. Scared? Sure. Why not?

Next day we reached Kwai Uen on the West River. I loaded all my cargo aboard a big river towboat pulled by a steam launch. That night I slept on a bunk near a window about fourteen inches square. A north wind blew in all night across my knees, but I was so exhausted that I didn't know it. Several times the next day, we had air raids. Each time our boat pulled beside the bank, and passengers scattered among the hills and gullies. Each time as I ran, one knee popped as if it were breaking. For years afterwards, it was so sore that I walked like a fellow with one leg. What joy to arrive safely in Wuchow with my last cargo of medicine!

Back in Wuchow it fell my lot to rebuild our Waang To Girls' School that I had built originally many years before. A new roof was put on, windows and doors restored, some desks and beds replaced. The school reopened and carried on as before—training young women for service.

Following a big Jap bombing which destroyed about one third of Wuchow, thousands of people were left homeless and hungry. We built large soup kitchens at the rear of the Baptist church and cooked boiled rice soup with a few vegetables. People lined up in long rows in front of our hospital, as coolies carried ten gallons of soup at a time along the lines. Our church workers dipped out a ladle full for each man, woman, and child. Finally, I built a big soup kitchen in my backyard, where we cooked tons and tons of rice for these suffering, hungry multitudes who had lost all of their earthly possessions.

After Pearl Harbor, at which time Hong Kong was also lost to the Japanese, the need for sulfa drugs became critical. Dr. Wallace asked me to go to Kweilin, a ten-day round-trip journey, to hunt for sulfa. I found one bottle containing one thousand tablets of Sulfathiazole, for $3,250, U. S. currency. Lives of suffering patients in our hospital at Wuchow depended on it. Those were terrible days. After one big air raid, Dr. Wallace and his faithful doctors and nurses operated all day without stopping. He would not stop even to eat. At the end of the day I took some milk to him and made him drink it. His Chinese doctors and nurses would have laid down their lives for this great surgeon, if need be. No wonder the multitudes in Wuchow loved him.

With food scarce and of poor quality, my teeth were going bad. A Chinese dentist who did not know much about germs crowned one tooth for me. My face soon looked like a one-sided balloon. Dr. Wallace yanked off the crown for me and finally had to pull the unwanted tooth.

Later, my tongue began to swell and there were tiny red spots over it. Dr. Wallace said, "Parson, hit the road at once for the U. S. A. and get some food; you are beginning to starve to death." I hated to leave him there alone, but if I were going to starve to death on his hands, I had better get going. It had already been eight years since I had left America and was nearly five since I had seen my family. Hesitantly, I got ready to depart from my beloved Wuchow and her people. This had been home for nearly a quarter of a century.

# 8

# Hitchhiking Home

The only way out of China was by airplane, so I cut my baggage accordingly. I could not leave behind my movie camera and movie films. I had a huge jacket with large pockets fore and aft, from neck to knees. Into these I could put my cans of film, four hundred feet each. Of course, I wore this monstrous jacket only when I boarded the plane.

As my boat shoved upriver to Kweilin, a group of Christians stood on the bank of the river, waving handkerchiefs and singing *Tin-foo po-oo nei*, transliterated, "God will take care of you."

After a few days on this crowded towboat and an exciting train ride, I arrived safely in Kweilin. In the city of Lau Chow where I caught the train, I met a group of missionaries who had just flown in from India. Among these were M. W. Rankin, Jessie Green, and Auris Pender. I gave them my camping equipment.

In Kweilin many people were fleeing westward, ahead of Japanese armies approaching from the east. Mrs. Baker J. Cauthen was ill with pneumonia. Dr. Beddoe warned that if her other lung became infected, her condition would be very serious. The enemy was getting close to Kweilin, and if Mrs. Cauthen got worse it would be impossible to remove her from the city. The Cauthens decided to do what the apostle James had instructed Christians to do (5:14). They sent word to missionaries and Chinese Christians who believed in prayer for the sick to come to their home that afternoon. Two missionaries and two Chinese brethren came. The Lord heard our prayers. That night the fever left. The next day the U. S. Air Force flew Mrs. Cauthen to an army hospital in Kunming, where she was well cared for until able to proceed to America with her husband and children.

By this time the Jap army was getting very close. Dr. and Mrs. R. E. Beddoe were next to fly over the mountains to Kunming. B. L. Nichols and I were the only American Baptists still in Kweilin. We turned our whole Baptist property over to the United States Army. I also gave the Army Intelligence my complete road map of Japan. Brother Nichols decided to leave by plane and I by train.

At the railway station in Kweilin, baggage was piled up on the platform in one pile about fifty feet long and twelve feet high. Some passengers piled on the car steps, while others climbed on top of the cars. One man had his table on top of the boiler; others had bicycles and other possessions tied to the outside of the cars. Still others had their earthly possessions piled on the cowcatcher, clinging onto it as the train pulled out. In Lau Chow we caught a mixed train out to the Northwest. Some passengers riding on top of cars were scraped to their death as the trains rushed into the first tunnel through the stone mountain.

During my five days on this horrible train I got desperate for sleep. My fellow passenger got off the end of our car seat, which was barely long enough for two, and I flopped down flat on my back, with my feet sticking out of the tiny window. They might have been knocked off, but when one reaches a certain stage of exhaustion he often takes chances with real danger.

At the end of this rail journey, we rushed for a Chinese army truck that was ready to take off toward Kwai Yeung, our next stop. Four of us missionaries—one an English lady —piled into the back of the truck on top of scanty baggage. We paid the truck driver holdup prices for our promised two-day ride, for wheels rolling under us was better than being left stranded in the mountains. Many times as our truck swayed around precipices, we wondered if we would crash in the bottom of those rugged canyons. Sometimes the truck driver killed the engine on a steep mountain grade, and the only way he could start the motor again was to let the truck roll backwards and then suddenly throw the thing into gear—while we listened for the gears to strip! With a deep canyon on each side, this little feat was hair-raising. But the Lord heard our prayers for the truck, the driver, and ourselves. At last we drove into Kwai Yeung, where we saw thousands of fleeing Chinese refugees—homeless, hungry, and weary.

At a missionary compound, an American doctor took a look at my tongue and said, "You had better keep going toward some good food in the U.S.A. You are still in starvation condition."

For five days I searched frantically for a way to travel, for I knew there had to be a way.

At last I found Arch McMillan, the son of a Southern Baptist missionary, driving a charcoal-burning truck for the Friends' Ambulance Corps. We wobbled along the war-worn roads, chugging and puffing up and down mountains, for a day and a night. In one town early in the morning we saw the Chinese army loading up to move on. Soldiers who had died during the night were stacked beside the road like cord wood. Along came the U. S. army. Their gasoline-fed trucks were making far more speed than our charcoal-burner, so I told Arch that I would hail them for a ride. The captain told me to pile in. He didn't have to tell me twice. I rode all that day in the back of a truck loaded with American soldiers, in the middle of a long convoy of army trucks. Those American truck drivers were about as reckless as our Chinese drivers had been, but their vehicles were better equipped. We rushed down one high mountain at what seemed break-neck speed. I counted twenty-five hairpin turns. Hanging onto the back end of the truck seemed to me like hanging onto a big steer's tail, sailing around in a branding corral. When we reached camp that night our eyes, noses, and mouths looked like red mudballs, for we had roared all day in a fog of red dust kicked up by our trucks. Shower baths were never so welcome!

The next day found me aboard a little narrow-gauge train that bounced along like a Texas jack rabbit. About dark we were unloaded in the cold, slushy streets of Kunming. Here I located Dr. and Mrs. Beddoe, my old friends of Wuchow. Sleeping on an army cot that night under woolen bankets in August was a restful experience in that high altitude.

The American consul issued me a new passport. The U. S. army gave me a pass on an airplane over "the Hump" into India, in part payment for the tent I had turned over to them. I had always thought that I would never ride in an airplane, but it was fly over "the Hump" or remain in China. About daylight I was at the airfield. After being weighed, together with all my movie films, I climbed aboard that freighter plane and zoomed away toward the highest mountains on earth.

My fellow passengers were three U. S. pilots going home for a vacation—all youngsters about twenty or twenty-one who had been matching their wits and bullets against the Japs for more than a year. Over Burma they pointed out where the Americans and Chinese were fighting the Japs miles below us in the jungles. And high up in the sky, we were in danger of being attacked any minute by Jap planes. By this time my flying partners were all rolled up in their furs and snoozing soundly, while I was left alone with the freezing cold to do the jitterbug worrying. I finally got my movie camera out and began shooting movies of mountains and clouds speeding by.

Suddenly we glided out over scenes hidden from mortal beings. Could this be the eternal garden of the gloryland? There was an endless vista of snowy billows, giant boulders, towering pillars. Everything sparkled and glittered in the light of the evening sun, unhampered by the dust and smoke of earth. Truly it seemed that we had ascended into the highest heavens and were beholding the glory of the Lord. Could heaven itself reflect any more of his majesty? Sailing on, we went around a cloud above and ahead of us that was sprinkling the silvery clouds below it with dewdrops.

Then we bade farewell to that gloryland and went out over the precipice to behold the jungles and great tea plantations of northeast Assam. As we drew nearer and nearer to earth, the tea plantations looked like garden spots sprinkled into the great wilderness of trees.

The next day I thumbed a plane ride to Calcutta, where I went to the American Express office and asked for a ship home. I told them that I would ride anything floating, provided it was going toward the U. S. A. Then I paid my fare for a Liberty ship that was to sail in a week.

In Calcutta, I observed more poverty, filth, and misery than I had ever seen in China. Thieving crows cluttered the air with their noise. They would actually fly into the houses and take food off the tables. My trigger finger itched to help these poor people get rid of the filthy airborne thieves. But kill one of these robbers? Oh, no, you don't! You are in India now!

An eclipse of the sun occurred while I was there. According to one of their false religions, all who washed in the Ganges River that day could wash away all their sins. I went to the river and saw thousands of people dipping themselves in the muddy waters. How much they needed to know that water—muddy or clear—could not wash away their sins! Jesus alone can save.

On Sunday morning I visited the very church where William Carey had preached more than a hundred years ago. I stood within a few inches of where that great missionary Adoniram Judson and his fearless wife, Ann Hasseltine Judson, were buried with Christ in baptism. (Ann's saintly, sacrificial life has done more to encourage me to fight on as a missionary than any other influence, aside from the Bible itself.)

Finally with my few clothes and movie films, I was aboard the S. S. *Amidon,* bound for America. Down the Hoogla River we steamed. At the mouth we joined a convoy of twenty ships, for in this area we were in danger of Japanese subs. A Liberty ship just behind the S. S. *Amidon* had been hit by a torpedo and was never heard of again. The name "Coffin Corner" was given to the left rear corner of a convoy. Whatever ship was assigned to this deadly corner took its place with no questions asked.

At Ceylon we went ashore for a day of seeing the wonders of that island. The next day our captain decided not to wait for a convoy across the Arabian Sea, a distance of about two thousand miles. When we were a thousand miles from nowhere except the bottom of the sea, the emergency alarm sounded. People rushed to the lifeboats as the captain yelled, "Submarine in the vicinity! Submarine in the vicinity!" The waves were rolling high. I thought, What's the use of getting into that turbulence? Just as well kiss ourselves good-bye and go down with the ship. But the Lord kept us safe, and on we steamed. If we could reach the Red Sea, we would be safe from submarines, for the British were supposed to have cleaned them out of the Red Sea and bottled it up at each end.

Late one afternoon we came to one of the most heart-thrilling sights of my life. Off to the east was Mount Sinai—a giant red mountain amid the desert sands. I could imagine the cloud of glory that gathered round when God himself came and talked things over with Moses for forty days and nights. Little wonder Moses' face shone. I could picture also the Israelites assembled at the foot of that glorious Mount, dancing, shouting, and parading around their glittering golden calf.

Farther north, my soul again stood at attention before the very trail the Israelites had traveled long ago. A swarm of large yellow grasshoppers came floating through the air from Egypt, and many fell upon the decks of our ship, reminding me of the plague of locusts the Lord had sent to that ancient empire.

Looking across the desert sands and hills of Egypt toward the setting sun, I could almost see a great cloud of red dust, with Pharaoh himself at the head of an angry army.

Then I realized that our ship was passing over the surface of Israel's trail and the silent watery grave of old Pharaoh and his armies.

After coming through the north end of the Suez Canal, we found our ship to be one among many flying American and British flags. Every ship was armed from bow to stern with all manner of antiaircraft guns. About dark the Germans gave us an air raid. Immediately the city of Port Said was blacked out in a smoke barrage. All the guns on shore and on ships turned loose everything they had. Talk about noise, we had it! No one had informed our ship's three hundred caged monkeys about air raids. But their screaming protests were soon drowned out by the barking guns. All this, plus shell fragments falling on steel decks, caused complete bedlam.

Since our ship was to anchor for three days in Port Said, some of us hired an old car and headed across the sandy spaces to Cairo to see the pyramids. At the foot of the hills we met some Arabs with their dromedaries for hire. These desert speedsters all had Bible names—my camel was "Moses." Great guy! I had ridden broncs, yes, but to stay in the saddle as Moses got up from his knees was almost impossible. I told the fellow leading Moses to let me have the lead rope; I wanted to do my own riding. I kicked old Moses some-where on his sides with my heels and gave the loudest cowboy yell I had in stock. He took off like a desert storm—and I wasn't sure it was one I could stop. After his first scare, how-ever, Moses didn't seem any more interested in physical exer-tion than the natives.

As our guide explained the ancient wonders of the pyra-mids and the Sphinx, he called it the "Spinkus." That be-came our name for him for the rest of the day. In the pyramids, through musty dungeons and dark hallways into gloomy, foul-smelling boneyards, were the mummified earthly pilgrims of ages past. I almost wondered whether "spooks" might jump out of those very much dried-up citizens of Pharaoh's day and claim me for a side partner to await the resurrection morn. I felt fresher and much safer out in God's open air again.

Our sight-seeing ended, we became all ears and eyes again, alert for a sound or sight of German subs and bombers. We felt a bit safer in a convoy, sailing toward Gibraltar. In a convoy one can always expect another ship to be hit instead of his own.

One Sunday afternoon our ship came near the island of Malta. It was time for our preaching service. The boys as-sembled and I read to them the Scriptures about Missionary Paul's experiences at sea in those very same waters, how nearly two thousand years ago Paul was aboard a ship with sailors and soldiers being tossed to and fro in a storm. I reminded them that here we were—missionary, sailors, and soldiers—on a ship nearing the same island. On Paul's journey they were shipwrecked in a terrific storm. We were in danger of being blown out to sea by a German submarine.

We sailed on near the shores of Italy and Sicily to Gibraltar, that mighty stone mountain. Here seventy-five ships gathered in convoy and made ready to dash through the gateway into the Atlantic Ocean. This was the most dangerous spot, because German subs would have opportunity to get us. Our air defenders had a big blimp and scout planes, searching for subs, hovering over us like a hen covering her chicks. When we were far out to sea, they left us and returned to land.

For many days our convoy zigzagged across the high seas. Here the navy "greyhounds of the sea" were our defenders, chasing around us like dogs herding sheep. As we dodged here and there, I prayed much for the seventy-five ships and their crews. Continuously these sailors and soldiers were on watch at their guns. All through the weary miles of days and nights, we heard our navy "greyhounds" dropping depth bombs at what they thought were attacking submarines. Christopher Columbus and his boys didn't have anything on us for joy and excitement when we finally saw the lights along the shores of America. Our watchful Lord heard our prayers for a safe journey!

When we were three days from land, we were just outside a terrible hurricane that swept the whole eastern coast of the United States.

After our ship dropped anchor, all eyes glistened with happiness that we were home again. But a somber note crept in when we saw along the sandy shore the ships blown out of the ocean by the storm.

"When do we land?" began going the rounds. At the end of five days of anxious waiting, our ship was ordered back east into German sub-infested seas. Having been within swimming distance of the shore and to have to go back into danger was more than we could understand. We didn't get blasted on our eastward journey, however, and soon we turned about-face, heading toward Savannah, Georgia. After two more days of anxious sea travel, our war-weary ship entered the mouth of the river.

My heart went up in thanksgiving to our Heavenly Father for answering our prayers for a safe journey. I had been on the way home for three and a half months, always in danger of Japanese or German warplanes and submarines. I am grateful to God for his care.

What a treat, I had thought, to buy a new pair of shoes! My own had long since been resoled with automobile tires—durable, but hardly in fashion for the grand homecoming. My stylish ambitions were short-lived, squelched by a curt demand for ration stamps. Ration stamps? What are they? I decided to start a new style.

This was summer, 1944. From Savannah I called my wife and heard her voice for the first time in nearly four years. She and our two girls were at home in Texas. God had taken care of my little family while I was in China, but both our boys had gone to war. After a few days my train rolled into Bonham ahead of schedule, and I surprised them. Mrs. Ray had bought us a little home that I had never seen, but my taxi driver took me right to it. It was the end of a nine-year journey around the world! I was met at the door by my little Mary Dee, whom I had not seen for about five years. I would not have known her had I met her elsewhere.

My first task was to enjoy food with real vitamins in it. Mrs. Ray and the girls took special delight in seeing "Pop" eat. Soon pounds were added, and I was ready to hit the highways, making speeches about China and showing moving pictures of our work there.

For eighteen months, I traveled in Kentucky, Missouri,

Oklahoma, and Texas. I accepted every speaking engagement possible, each time pouring out my heart to help Southern Baptists see the great need.

War guns finally ceased rumbling in Germany and Japan. Shattered armies and nations found time then to bury their dead, clear away the ruins of cities and homes, and begin planning for a brighter future. It was a happy time when David and Dan came home from the battlefields of Leyte, Okinawa, and Korea; and my brother, Chaplain Dave Ray, came home from Germany, where he had served with Patton's Fourth Armored Division. Praise the Lord!

The time passed quickly, with many speaking trips. In the spring we proudly saw our two daughters graduate—Lois from high school and Mary Dee from grammar school.

Once more, and for the last time, I began packing to go back to China. Son Daniel and nephew David Hicks loaded about a ton of medical supplies, relief clothing, and baggage on our trailer for the trip to San Francisco. I said, "Good-bye, darling wife and daughters. See you again in years to come," and we were gone.

For three days and nights Hicks, Dan, and I took turns driving, for a railway strike was on, and I simply had to catch my ship at San Francisco. Our top-heavy trailer acted as its own speed regulator; the instant we passed the forty-mile-an-hour mark, the trailer wobbled dangerously! In San Francisco we rushed to get a ticket and bills of lading, then crated and hauled the trailer's contents to the shipping wharves. "Good-bye, Sonny Boy Dan and David Hicks! God be with you till we meet again!" They turned their faces toward Texas, and I looked far away to seething China. On a Friday the thirteenth in 1946 our ship *Marine Lynx*, just released by the army, slipped out into the great Pacific toward the mysterious Orient.

At sea, the engineers discovered that someone had filled

the boilers with salt water. For days, we sailed on one boiler at a time, while the crew cleaned out the salt. The fog whistle blew most of the time from San Francisco to the southern tip of Japan. Ours was the first ship to sail from the United States to Hong Kong via Shanghai since World War II ended. We had many Chinese passengers traveling third-class, returning to China after years of gathering American dollars. Some lost their lifetime savings at gambling tables on the ship. Others were to lose theirs at the hands of Chinese bandits before they reached their native villages.

On Sundays on the ship, Protestants and Baptists worshiped together, but Catholics wouldn't even worship with each other. Each different kind set up his own little altar in a different part of the room. But when we get to heaven, all the redeemed of the Lord will bow humbly at his feet and join *together* in the alleluias.

Missionary Eugene Hill was on the wharf at Kowloon, Hong Kong, waving hands of welcome to us—Mrs. Hill and son John, Misses Shumate, Pender, Pettigrew, and myself. Since this was the first ship from America to enter port after the war, nothing was organized to handle the many passengers and the baggage cargo. We spent three days hunting lost items.

I spent another four days trying to find a way to Wuchow. All the river steamers had been lost during the war. Finally, I got my relief supplies, baggage, and portable organs aboard a greasy oil junk. After three days and nights of roosting on various sizes of freight boxes and cargo, we gladly hustled ashore at Wuchow. I delivered part of the medical supplies and one organ to Stout Memorial Hospital, then loaded the rest on a big Chinese towboat headed upriver to Lau Chow, en route to Kweilin. The boat was packed and jammed with cargo, Chinese passengers, smoke, and smells. I had to come up for fresh air now and then, or suffocate. At Lau Chow, a

Britisher distributing relief goods in forty Dodge and Ford trucks loaned me a two-ton truck to move my goods to Kweilin. On the second day of truck travel, August 13, 1946, I unloaded my relief goods, medical supplies, and earthly possessions in the ruins of Kweilin Baptist Hospital.

# 9
# Rebuilding

I set up my cot in the corner of a former hospital room, a folding dining table and camp stove under a tree. Here my Chinese-boy cook, A Wing, and I started housekeeping—or camping—in a city that was about 96 per cent destroyed in the Japanese war.

The Baptist church, hospital, schools, Bible school, and missionary residence were just masses of burned brick walls and ruins. Thieves were already tearing down and carrying away thousands of bricks. With the help of the police, I recovered part of these.

Since the Japanese invaders had left, women, girls, boys, and men began clearing-up operations. Foxholes, dugouts, and air-raid shelters were leveled; masses of six-foot grass and weeds were removed. Then rebuilding began.

First, two small rooms in the Bible school were repaired for temporary living quarters. Materials were bought and work begun on the Baptist church and its Sunday school rooms. Funds for the original building, and again for the rebuilding of the church, were given largely by Miss Laura Powers of Knoxville, Tennessee, in memory of her father. (Later, her liberal gifts helped this cowboy missionary to carry on the Lord's work in Korea.) At the same time the Kweilin Baptist Church was being rebuilt, the Baptist hospital was partially restored and the missionary residences were made into apartment houses for those missionaries who were to come later. Baptist church buildings in the country also were repaired or rebuilt.

Then came the happy hour when reinforcements began to arrive: Brother Deaver Lawton came in September, 1946, weary and worn by train and truck travel from Hong Kong. In January, 1947, Mrs. Lawton, their two children, and Miss Mildred Lovegren arrived by airplane from Canton. A year later, my wife arrived safely by train through bandit-infested areas between Canton and Kweilin. One bitter cold night on that train Mrs. Ray, laced up in a sleeping bag, dreamed that bandits were attacking and she couldn't get out of the bag. Never since has she been persuaded to try a sleeping bag. Later we welcomed Brother Oz Quick and his wife Mary into our repossessing-staff of missionaries in Kweilin.

Greatest and most important of all our work was the spiritual revival and renewal of hope in the hearts of Chinese Baptists. Street preaching began in the sheltered corners of the buildings under reconstruction. Multitudes of Chinese —rich and poor—were now anxious to hear the gospel. Many heard and believed on the Lord Jesus Christ. Bible classes and gospel preaching began in the high schools and in Kwong Sai University. One hundred university students were enrolled in one Bible class taught by the missionaries. Another Bible class for the university teachers was begun—twenty-two professors joined. The demand for Bibles was greater than we could supply. One cold winter night 225 high school students walked four miles to hear the eternal gospel preached by Dr. Baker J. Cauthen. Nearly all of them accepted Jesus that night. The next night, four hundred students walked over the same rough roads to hear Dr. Cauthen, and many of them accepted Christ.

When the Baptist Hospital at Kweilin was ready to reopen, we had no medical staff. Then we received a telegram that the entire staff of the Baptist hospital in Cheung Cho, in central China, was coming to join us. Soon Dr. Ayers and his staff moved in and assumed responsibilities.

They were almost ready to open the doors when a telegram came from Miss Lovegren and our missionary nurse, who had been in a bus wreck south of Kweilin. Dr. Ayers, Brother Quick, and I piled into our truck and rushed to their rescue, through the night, in a cold March rain. We arrived about midnight. Dr. Ayers and Brother Quick bound up wounds and broken bones as best they could, then loaded the most seriously injured patients into the back of the truck. The tarp and curtains were pulled taut to keep out rain and cold. Dr. Ayers and Brother Oz stayed in there with the moaning victims. Only a pump kerosene lantern was available to keep them from freezing.

To our horror, we discovered that gasoline and water do not work together in the same carburetor. I spread a tarp over the hood and cleaned out the water by flashlight. The truck ran a short distance, and the operation had to be repeated. After so much grinding, the battery finally died. We could do nothing but pray and wait for daylight while Dr. Ayers comforted his groaning patients through the rest of the night.

When morning came, a large crowd of coolies gathered around us, but their demands for pay were too high. Another crowd came along. After much bargaining, they consented to give us a push to start our motor. It was a severe test of faith, trying to persuade men to help their own wounded people. Finally, our motor sputtered a few times and then we took off toward Kweilin and our Baptist hospital. In all my years of driving, never had I rejoiced more to hear a motor start doing its duty!

About eleven o'clock in the morning, we drove up to the hospital. White-robed nurses and doctors took over the care of that truckload of wounded patients!

In Lau Chow I received from U. N. N. R. A. several truck-loads of medical supplies, food and clothing, mosquito netting, and one truckload of powdered milk. These were divided among Kweilin Baptist Hospital, Stout Memorial Baptist Hospital in Wuchow, and Tai Kam Baptist Leper Hospital on the southern coast of China. I also distributed needed supplies among the Baptist churches around Kweilin.

A big riverboat was loaded with medical supplies for the hospital in Wuchow and the leper colony, together with our few earthly possessions. We said "Good-bye and God bless you all" to the Ayerses, Quicks, Lawtons, and Miss Lovegren, and to many Chinese Baptists waving their hands along the shore. Then our twelve boatmen leaned against their oars and the boat glided into the Foo River and headed downstream toward Wuchow. Our assignment to "rebuild the walls of Kweilin" was accomplished. We turned now toward the future.

After a few days of riding the crested floodwaters of the Foo River, we pulled up along the riverbanks of Wuchow. We got some of the mission property titles in order and turned them over to Dr. Wallace. Mrs. Ray and I visited the home where four of our children were born and where we had spent some twenty years of our lives. It tore our hearts to turn away from it forever.

As we said, "Farewell, Dr. Bill," little did we know it was for the last time. William Wallace joined the martyrs in heaven in February, 1951.

With our belongings aboard a big junk, we were towed downriver toward Toi Shan and Tai Kam Leper Colony, our last stand in our beloved China. As we passed through the bandit-infested areas, Mrs. Ray and I went down into the hold of the boat, below the waterline, to be jammed in between stacks of cargo. It was better to be safely uncomfortable than comfortable and full of bullet holes. The Lord saw us safely through, and we relaxed as we moved ashore to a rented apartment in Toi Shan.

One hundred boxes of medical and other relief supplies came in with us. We had transferred the lot six different times from truck to boats and from those boats to other boats. Before we could begin unpacking, the worst typhoon and flood in thirty years roared in. For forty-eight hours it swooshed us about in its fury, making the nearby river a little ocean and our hilltop house an island before the winds and slashing rain abated.

In Toi Shan there was not a Baptist or Protestant missionary. One group of Chinese Baptists told us they had been praying the Lord would send some missionaries, and they felt that Mrs. Ray and I were the answer. Our upstairs apartment needed 120 windowpanes, but we were happy to have a place to call home.

We helped to rebuild the Baptist church in Toi Shan. There was great rejoicing among the Chinese Christians when we reopened and rededicated the building for the preaching of the gospel! Mrs. Ray was soon busy organizing and training the new choir and Training Union. We were encouraged to see young people who had come through the war now anxious to carry on for the Lord.

The pastor and I visited Tai Kam Leper Colony, the first visit by anyone since Japanese invasion. I mounted the baggage carrier on the rear of a bicycle, while the Chinese bicycleman pedaled me across country for thirty miles! Then we walked over the mountain to a village where I preached in a new Baptist chapel. That night we rowed across the open sea to the leper colony and hospital on Tai Kam Island.

Just before sunrise we dropped anchor. I blew a big conk-shell horn. The lepers on shore responded by singing songs of praise to the Lord. It was glorious music, coming from the hearts of lepers who were anxiously awaiting our arrival. This experience made me think of the time ahead when my little bark will drop anchor on eternity's shore, where I shall hear voices of the redeemed welcoming me home from my last voyage.

There were only three survivors out of more than a hundred lepers on the island when the Japanese attacked. After happy greetings, Brother Ng and I went with the lepers to the church building for a service. Benches and chairs were gone, but the lepers still had their songbooks. After the Japanese had left, Chinese pirates came to loot and carry away everything loose—doors, windows, furniture, and equipment. In all our buildings—church, hospital, fourteen dormitories, and administration buildings—not a thing was left.

Tai Kam Island had been given to Baptists by the Chinese government, through Wu Ting Fong, ambassador to the United States. Brother and Sister John Lake had built the colony well; now it was my task to start "rebuilding the walls" of Tai Kam for the lepers. Returning to the mainland of China, I purchased materials and equipment and hired carpenters. We carried the rehabilitation program to completion in the summer of 1948.

Pirates—seventy-five families of them—lived on the opposite side of the island. When I visited and preached to them, they were friendly and interested in the Lord's message. A fine Christian young man on the Mainland offered to teach in the Baptist School for Pirates' Children, which I organized. (I drew up a contract which I still hold.) Boys filled the tiny schoolroom by day. The girls attended at night, because they had to work on the mountains and in the tiny fields during the day. On my last visit with the pirates, they begged me to come and build a church for them.

About this time the Chinese navy, in pursuit of the pirates, surrounded Tai Kam and gave the whole island a bad shelling and machine-gunning.

A year later, in the summer of 1949, the Lord answered our prayers for a doctor to take over and manage the leper hospital and colony. Dr. Joshua Yeung and his wife, a trained nurse, accepted our invitation and came to Toi Shan, temporarily making their home with us. Then we moved most of his baggage and a lot of medical supplies to Chek Kai Chapel on the seashore, where Dr. Yeung and I stayed, ready to board our boat for the leper colony.

Just after midnight we were awakened by two battering rams beating down the chapel door. When I went downstairs to open it, there were four hooded bandits, four flashlights, and four pistols staring me in the face. No doubt a tall, gangling, bald-headed missionary, scantily dressed in white nightclothes, looked ghostly to them. Anyway, they ordered me to sit on a front bench and then bound my arms behind me with rope. The bandit who stood just in front of me, his pistol pointed at my heart, kept saying in Chinese, "Don't move or I'll kill you! Don't move or I'll kill you!" All the time his gun-hand was shaking as though he had the palsy. Dr. Yeung was hit on the arm with a bandit's pistol, and the Chinese pastor was struck on the head with another.

When the bandits finished their looting, they ordered us to close the door after them and keep very quiet. We did. Then we looked around to see what was missing. My reliable watch, movie camera, eyeglasses, about ten dollars in cash, raincoats, leather traveling bag and contents, seven woolen blankets for the lepers, and most of Dr. Yeung's earthly possessions had departed to be with their new owners. Praise the Lord, they did not take our medical supplies!

Back in the mountains, the bandits fought over their stolen goods. The usual results: one of them pushing up daisies. I doubt that his funeral was very elaborate. Later, I found the bandits and handed over more cash to redeem my eyeglasses, movie camera, and New Testament, and Dr. Yeung's diplomas. (A doctor could not practice medicine in China without his diplomas.) The bandit chief invited Dr. Yeung to visit them in the mountains and administer to their sick, and he did. The bandits even wanted him to remain with them and be their doctor.

Whenever Mrs. Ray and I sojourned with the lepers, we lived in a special little house built by Brother Lake. One evening I came into my dining room at the leper colony and found I had company. The pirates had come and stacked their guns on my table. Friendly boys they were. They cooked their supper in my kitchen. After supper I suggested that I make their pictures. They were happy to have them made, so I took both movies and still pictures of them and of myself with their machine gun. Then they loaded their shooting irons into their rowboats and headed for the high seas to continue their work of pirating helpless ships.

One day the pirates' wives and daughters came over the mountains to visit us there. They had climbed for miles over those rugged mountains to be with us in our last farewells on the island. They brought Mrs. Ray presents of peanuts and dried fish to show their thankfulness for our work among them. We assembled all our visitors in the shade of our house and preached the gospel to them. Mrs. Ray taught them to sing about Jesus.

It was "farewell" to lepers, to pirates, and to the Yeungs. We had a happy time introducing Dr. and Mrs. Yeung and their little girl to the lepers. Now we turned the work over to them completely and set sail across the high seas to finish our work in Toi Shan.

# 10

# The Doors of China Close

The Red armies were approaching Canton rapidly. On October 13, 1949, I attended the last Leung Kwong Baptist Convention ever held in Free China. After the night service, Dr. Belote and I rushed to the wharf in a jeep; but the last ship had already sailed, ahead of schedule, and six airplanes had taken off for the last time to Hong Kong. Only one hope of escape remained—a last train early the next morning for Hong Kong, before the Communists took Canton. I was at the railway station an hour before the train was due to leave. The train was there, tickets all sold, and already enough people and baggage stuffed into the cars to fill three trains. At last I found a black market ticket, at double the right price. I bought it and climbed over people and baggage to my supposed seat underneath more people and baggage. I roosted on top. When trainmen came through the car, they walked on the backs of the seats. Some Chinese soldiers wanted to put their wives aboard, so I pulled four of them through the window, while their husbands pushed from the outside. The husbands were left to suffer their fate. It was a great relief when our train crossed the border into British territory. Wonderful freedom! God help Americans to cherish and protect it!

Mrs. Ray was in Toi Shan alone, and I felt that I *must* return there before the Reds took that city also. All Hong Kong boats to Toi Shan had stopped running. In Macao I found a little freight junk going to Kong Moon, which was on the road home. Before we arrived, however, the captain got scared that his boat might be commandeered and turned back to Macao. I found a way overland to Kong Moon, but it was full of fleeing nationalist troops. They had commandeered every bus and boat to help move their retreating armies, and it looked as though I might not make it home after all. Finally, after much searching, I found a hidden taxi, whose driver was willing to risk the trip for an exorbitant price. Ten of us were in and on that taxi. At the next town a soldier commandeered my private taxi and chased out all the Chinese passengers, even the driver and his mechanic. He tried to put me out also, but I refused to move an inch. He got hold of my suitcase, but I held on with all my strength, and we had a tug-of-war. All the while I was yelling, "I must see the General." He finally gave up and permitted my driver and mechanic to get back in. Maybe the soldier decided that I was a general! Anyway, he filled the car with soldiers and we proceeded. We passed thousands of weary, sick soldiers in their sad retreat. Many of them had their wives and a few babies with them. They were a long way from their northern homes.

Later a Chinese army officer stopped us and ordered all my soldier passengers out. Then he told me in perfect English that he had spent a year in the U. S. A. I told him I was glad to give his boys a ride, but he replied, "No, they have got to walk." So once more my driver, the mechanic, and I were on our way—this time without any passengers. At the end of the journey I paid my fare, crossed the river, and caught a bus to Toi Shan where Mrs. Ray was anxiously awaiting my return. How thankful I was to the Lord just to be home again, though not for long.

Too late now to escape! Fleeing nationalist soldiers had taken all the trucks and busses in their last flight toward the seacoast. There was nothing for us to do but to wait patiently for the Lord. Merchants had moved all their valuables to the country for hiding. One night a bus, a private car, and a jeep loaded with Red soldiers entered the city. They captured it without firing a shot. For many weeks the China war had been only a footrace, with nationalists fleeing and Reds trying to catch them. The nationalist soldiers stayed too long in Toi Shan, squeezing money out of the people. They missed the boat that was sent to receive them at a designated place on the seacoast. The Reds backed them up against the sea and took the whole lot of them prisoner, along with their loot. I stood at the roadside for half an hour watching the Red captors march their prisoners by, while throngs of school-children (under orders) stood beside the road, waving their new Red flags and yelling, "Hurrah for the liberating army and down with Chiang Kai-shek!"

All the "liberating" the Red army did in Toi Shan was to open the prison doors and turn the jailbirds loose on the public again. The next day those ex-prisoners were wandering through the streets gazing at us as we went to church. I went ahead and preached the gospel, however, as though there were no Reds in the place. For the next eighteen days everything around us was in such a state of unrest and uncertainty that Mrs. Ray and I decided to get out of China, if we could, before the Reds got too curious about us. Then, too, the new government had enlisted hundreds of pirates and bandits and put them in charge to "protect" the city. The citizens became uneasy. Their faith in these bandit-protectors was not very strong!

Another act of the new "liberators" was to relieve the Girls' Normal School treasury of thirty thousand dollars in Hong Kong currency. "Liberation," indeed, from "capitalist lucre"! Even though the school had supposedly joined the Reds, the American-trained lady superintendent of eighteen years' experience was kicked out, and a boy who was not even a high school graduate was installed as the new superintendent. The other teachers could not resign—they had to teach at the equivalent of sixteen cents U. S. currency per day. People began to realize the Red "liberators" were not what they had represented themselves to be, but it was too late!

We realized that our continued presence in China would endanger the lives of our Christian brothers and sisters. Our Christian neighbor, a lady schoolteacher, had taught the ruling Red "boss" in our city when he was a boy, and, as far as she was concerned, he was still her schoolboy. On our behalf, she visited his office and asked for a permit for Mrs. Ray and me to leave China and take our baggage out without inspection. He granted the permit as requested. We divided our goods with Dr. Yeung and loaded the rest of our belongings (which included a well hidden radio) into a small rented bus. Then we said our last good-bye to Christian friends on the mainland of China.

Mrs. Ray boarded the bus with our stuff, and I escorted the bus on my motorcycle. Armed with the Red boss's permit, we dashed for the seacoast. Each time Red soldiers stopped us, I drew out my Red permit and showed it. It had a very quieting effect. When we get to heaven, I want to thank that little Chinese woman for that permit.

At the seacoast, we loaded our baggage on a sixty-foot motorboat, due to make the attempted run to Macao. If we could reach Macao, we would be *free* again. The Red soldiers minutely examined each Chinese passenger and every scrap of paper he had, but when I showed my permit, they passed us and our baggage without a look. At the "all clear" signal, we sailed out into beautiful moonlit waters—but not for long. One engine broke down, and we were forced to return to port for repairs.

The next day, having repaired the engine, we were examined again very thoroughly by a new set of Reds. This time they would not accept my permit. I had to go ashore and visit the local magistrate. I'm sure the Lord gave me the right words to speak. I reminded this Red official how I had recently treated one of his wounded soldiers during a battle around our chapel on the seacoast at Chek Kai. He remembered. I also told him that many years ago I helped entertain the "Father of China," Dr. Sun Yat-sen, and had my picture made with him. Within a few minutes all was well again, and we sailed once more for the high seas. I was very anxious to get clear of Red territory, lest they change their minds.

Soon our sputtering engines had us out into free waters. This thought was comforting, even though wild waves were tossing our little craft in all directions. Most of the passengers and crew were soon "feeding the fish," but for once I escaped seasickness.

As we passed Tai Kam Island Leper Colony, we saw Dr. Yeung. He was in a boat that was flying the Red Cross flag. The guards, fearing that every boat was loaded with pirates, were about to fire on Dr. Yeung. I jumped into action, yelling, "What do you mean, preparing to fire on a boat flying the Red Cross flag? Don't you know that is against international law?" An ignorant man with a rifle in his hands is dangerous, on the borders of Russia or in any other nation.

In Macao at last, the police disarmed our guards and permitted us to go ashore. Praise God, we were free once more! We learned that, on its return to China, our little boat was lost in the storm, and the thirteen passengers never saw land again. The Lord had wonderfully piloted us safely through.

Long ago he had promised, "When thou passest through the waters I will be with thee."

Soon Mrs. Ray and I were back in our little cottage on Cheung Chow Island, near Hong Kong. Truly "a house built upon rock," it stood on a high stone bluff overlooking the restful, glittering sea.

Before leaving China forever, we visited the Happy Valley Cemetery in Hong Kong. There among the lonely, whispering pines, we planted our last bouquet at the head of a grave with this inscription on beautiful stone: "Marian McNair Ray. Age 5. Daughter of Missionaries Rex and Janet G. Ray. Every Thing's All Right in My Father's House." We held no fear, for we knew that we would see our little daughter again in our Father's house.

Soon thereafter we boarded an American ship. As we moved slowly out of Hong Kong Harbor—past Kowloon railway station, the Peninsula Hotel, the crowded settlement area —and on toward the wide ocean, memories crowded our thoughts. Tears of joy, loneliness, and relief fell as we stood on deck, watching the many kinds of ships, junks, and sampans in the bay. Beyond them rose the tall mountain, with the city spread over its valleys and peaks. Memories of thirty years swept through our souls as we watched China fade away slowly into the setting sun. It was our last sunset in that dear old land.

After a long voyage in a stormy, turbulent ocean, we came to more peaceful waters along the snow-covered mountains of the great Pacific Northwest. Hopes revived, as our hearts thrilled to be again in our beloved America.

In Seattle we had a happy reunion with my brother Claude and his family. Our son David, who was in the army, also greeted us and traveled by train with us to visit my sister, Lynn Cox, in Grass Valley, California. In Berkeley we bought an ancient Studebaker and took David with us to behold the beauties of Yosemite National Park. Only our God can create such glorious wonders!

David returned to the army, and we headed "Stude" southward, through the fertile valleys, fields, and orchards of California. Turning east, we hurried across the bleak deserts of California, Arizona, New Mexico, and western Texas, until at last we came to Bonham—home sweet home! "Thank you, Lord, for your protection and guidance through all the years."

About dusk we rolled into the driveway at home, quickly changed clothes, and went to Bonham High School. The senior play was underway. At the close of the first act, Mrs. Ray said, "Didn't our baby girl act well?"

"Who? Was Mary Dee in the play?" I didn't even recognize her, after four years. How much she had grown! Now in May, 1950, she would graduate from high school. Son Daniel and daughter Lois would graduate from Baylor University— my alma mater.

Great joy filled our hearts to see and hear Lois give her own speech recital to a large audience before graduation. Then with some eight hundred others, Daniel and Lois received their degrees. Four years later Mary Dee followed in their footsteps, because God had moved the hearts of Southern Baptist women to provide the Margaret Fund to assist missionaries' children through school. Had it not been for this, our children could never have gone through college. God bless Woman's Missionary Union!

Daniel is now a Southern Baptist missionary in Korea. Lois is working with her husband in a boys' camp in Texas for the salvaging of disturbed boys. Mary Dee and her husband are working in Alaska, which she calls her "mission field."

# 11
# Korea Calling

Another year rushed into history. Mrs. Ray and I traveled all over our southland, showing pictures and telling of Southern Baptist mission work. Then it came—the urgent call of Korean Baptists: "Baptist missionaries, come over and help us!" John Abernathy was the only Baptist missionary then in Korea. The call stirred my soul.

November 18, 1951, with a new jeep and trailer loaded with hospital equipment and relief clothing, I left Bonham and Janet behind (the U. S. Army would not permit women to enter Korea). My cousin, Dr. John Ray, who was an American consul in Russia when that country fell into the hands of the Bolsheviks, traveled with me to San Francisco.

Across the western prairies, our jeep left the miles behind. We had a pleasant visit with my brother Dennis and family in Tucson, Arizona. Along the weary miles of desert roads, Cousin John did the talking as I piloted the jeep. Late one evening, he became silent after this remark, "Rex, my tongue is sore." In San Francisco, he boarded a bus for Texas, and I loaded my jeep and trailer aboard a freighter for Korea.

After having taken all the cholera, typhoid, and typhus

shots, I ambled aboard the ship. It was just getting dark as we glided under Golden Gate Bridge. Out in the open sea, our ship began to roll, as a severe storm struck from the west.

As our ship rolled, things really happened inside. Dishes in the dining saloon leaped into the air and crashed wherever they landed. My cabin was soon a wreck. Chairs turned somersaults; my trunk took off on its own without a pilot; the desk drawers rushed out and dumped their contents all over the floor. With my back against the wall and my knees against the side of my bunk, I tried to keep from making a flying tackle into mid-air for a landing against the opposite side of my cabin. My stomach did well. I didn't lose it. But food for the next two days and nights—don't mention it! At Seattle, I reached for land. I spent the night ashore at my brother Claude's. I couldn't work up any enthusiasm for launching out into the wild Pacific again.

Shortly before we were to sail, Janet called from Texas. My brother Don had suffered a stroke. It was a hard test— turn back to Texas or continue to Korea? Duty and lost souls of Korea called. I had to sail on and leave my brother in the loving hands of my Lord. Shortly thereafter he went to be with Jesus and our loved ones over there.

The stormy sea seemed ready and anxious to swallow us, ship and all. When it seemed I could stand no more, I prayed earnestly. The next day the raging billows calmed, and we sailed on toward war-torn Korea. Jesus still answers prayers according to his promises, and he still controls the wind and the waves. He is the best friend a saved sinner ever had.

We sailed around the north end of Japan. After a few days on the Sea of Japan, we dropped anchor just outside Pusan. I felt almost "at home" the next morning as the fog and smoke lifted and I saw a ship from Hong Kong nearby. The anchor chains then crawled back into the ship, bringing our anchor up out of the mud. Slowly in the morning hours our ship wound its way through the harbor and alongside the wharf.

On shore, welcoming me to Korea, were the waving hands and smiling faces of John Abernathy, Dr. N. A. Bryan (a "refugee" out of China), Brother and Sister David Ahn, and my future faithful assistant, Kim Kwong Hoon. Praise the Lord! At last I was in the land of Korea.

We soon got the jeep rolling on land but had to wait three days before I could get my baggage out of the hold. There were only twelve thousand bags of GI Christmas mail on top of it, December 1951! After a few days of talk-talk with the customs, my possessions were released, duty free.

The Lord had once more opened doors for me to witness for him. Warplanes were roaring in the skies, as bombs crashed on the battlefields in the north. Armies, trucks, and war materials were on the move day and night everywhere in South Korea. Literally millions of homeless refugees fled from the Communists in the north. Oh, that I might make Jesus known to many in this weary land!

To begin this evangelistic and relief work, Kwong Hoon and I loaded our jeep and trailer with food and clothing and started northward to Taegu. It was a thrilling experience for me to preach in an upper room filled with people. They were sitting on the floor in their stocking feet (we had all left our shoes outside the door—Korean custom). A preacher could never tire preaching to people so hungry to hear the gospel of our Lord Jesus! So it was all over South Korea.

We stayed in one home where the Saturday night bath was memorable. An iron barrel in a back shed was exposed to a roaring fire underneath and to a roaring blizzard just out of the North Pole. The shed had a few slats on the north side to break the force of the freezing winds. I don't know whether my host expected me to hit that barrel of super-hot water head-on or feet first. Neither appealed to me, so I called for more cold water. A few bucketfuls were added, and my host left me to cook or freeze. I had no desire to do either. Instead, I dipped out a small portion of the hot liquid and gently poured it on the north side, hoping the south side would not freeze while I was doing the north!

When war struck Korea, there were 150 churches in the Korean Baptist Convention. Of these, 110 were in the North and 40 in the South. What became of those in the North only the Lord knows. It was my duty to preach to as many of the churches in South Korea as I could.

Two years before the Japanese were driven out of Korea in 1945, the Japanese heard that these Baptists were preaching about the kingdom of God and about one Jesus Christ, King of kings and Lord of lords. So they called some Baptist preachers on the carpet about this doctrine, wanting to know where the Japanese emperor fitted into this kingdom. Those Baptist preachers told them, "If your emperor does not repent of his sins and believe on the Lord Jesus, he won't be in this kingdom at all." As a result, all Baptist preachers and some deacons in Korea were arrested and put in prison, where they stayed until the Japanese were kicked out of Korea. The president of the Korean Baptist Convention died in a Japanese prison.

Kwong Hoon and I continued our missionary travels. One cold night at a farm home, our host covered our jeep with bundles of rice straw to keep it from freezing. Everywhere we went, the brethren wanted to do all they could to help in our missionary work. They insisted on giving us the best portions of their food. What a joy to give them warm clothing sent from the U. S. A.

At Kang Kyung Baptist Church, on the western side of Korea, we preached in a building that had once been a Japanese heathen temple. We were entertained by the widow, son, and granddaughter of Pastor Lee. When Pastor Lee, then president of the Korean Baptist Convention, and a young deacon were being led away to be shot by the Communists, Pastor Lee told the deacon, "You make a break and run in the darkness. You might make it. I'm old and my work is nearly finished." Young Deacon Kim did escape, even though the Reds shot *at* him. According to one book, some four hundred preachers were murdered in Korea by the Communists.

On our way southwestward, a Korean pastor with us asked me to stop the jeep. He pointed across the field.

"See that village yonder? There is a Baptist church there whose members have been told that you are coming today."

As we looked, a stream of people came running across the fields toward us. They greeted us warmly. Then they stood beside the highway in icy winds and snow and listened earnestly and patiently to the gospel message. What a joy to witness for Jesus to hungry hearts!

In southwestern Korea, a large crowd gathered in a new Baptist church building and were seated on the floor. Forty people—old and young—accepted Jesus as their Saviour that night. We traveled on and on over South Korea. Everywhere people accepted Christ. Winter snows kept getting higher and higher around one country church far up in the mountains, but for three nights people came out of their little huts to hear more about Jesus. Ninety accepted him as Saviour and Lord.

At Kunsan, on the west coast, I preached to eight hundred prisoners, about five hundred of whom professed acceptance of Christ. Two of the prisoners were given pardons from President Syngman Rhee. It was a great hour for those men, but how much greater for those who accepted Jesus and received eternal pardons. At Kunsan, I also preached for a week at the U. S. Air Base. GIs and Koreans alike gave their hearts to the Lord Jesus.

I saw some of the heartaches that come to GIs. Boys in the ground forces equipped great bombers and fighter planes for their flights to the battlefronts above the thirty-eighth parallel. They would watch their buddies fly to the north with their loads of bombs and destruction. When the hour of return came and went without a sign of the planes, these boys knew their buddies would never return. With sad hearts they would go back to their barracks—the vacant bunks and the empty seats at the table—and grit their teeth, wondering what the next day would bring.

The chaplain would gather the missing pilots' few possessions and mail them back to the boys' homes, with letters telling loved ones their sons, husbands, or brothers would not be returning home.

In all our travels in Korea, American soldiers were anxious to help us. They kept my jeep in good repair and equipped with new tires.

As the Korean war went on and on, our preaching and relief mission also carried on and on. During March of 1953, we distributed twenty tons of clothing and fourteen tons of rice among the refugees in South Korea. Everywhere, people in the city and country churches begged me to remain. They felt that the preaching of the gospel was more important than distributing relief goods. They were right, but I felt that I should continue to do both. During my first eighteen months in Korea, I rested for one day—that was the day Dr. Bryan made me stay in bed with the flu.

Dr. Bryan had opened Baptist medical work at Pusan in a little army tent in the front yard of the First Baptist Church. He had six patients the opening day in December, 1951. The number of patients grew daily until a high of seven hundred was reached for one day. From January to April 25, 1953, Dr. Bryan and the nurses—Misses Wheat, Branum, and Wright—with their Korean helpers, gave 30,269 treatments to 9,260 patients, in two rooms ten by twelve feet. This medical service was given free through Southern Baptists' offerings for

Korean relief. The refugees were treated "without money and without price." Starving, sick children were transformed into healthy little people, with the help of vitamin tablets and powdered milk that Christians sent.

During these years, Dr. John Abernathy "drove like jehu" as he went about preaching to prisoners of war, baptizing, counseling Korean church leaders, building church buildings, serving as treasurer of the mission, conducting services for GIs, and serving as general information dispenser at Baptist headquarters. Mrs. Abernathy rushed back to him, as soon as the U. S. Army would permit, to help keep his soul and body together.

One night that winter icy winds out of the North swept man-trampled dust through the streets of Pusan. As the storm increased its fury, the lights blacked out. Five thousand people sat in darkness on straw mats on the ground, listening earnestly to Evangelist Billy Graham's message about the rich young man who wanted eternal life but wasn't willing to pay the price. When the loud speaker quit, Billy's voice could still be heard under the cold Korean stars. More than six hundred people responded to the invitation and accepted Christ as Saviour. Some were GIs. The fight for things eternal is on in Korea.

Kim Kwong Hoon answered the call to preach the gospel. For three months I worked with Mike Chiu, my new assistant. We started distributing fifteen tons of clothing. One night we stopped at an inn where a little orphan girl was working. After she had wiped the floor of our tiny room clean, so we could lay down our sleeping bags for the night, she told us the war had destroyed her home and parents and left her and her little brother homeless. When she finished her heartbreaking story, I decided to use some Southern Baptist relief money. Her thin little face broke into a smile as she said, "Now I have enough money to buy a shirt for my little brother." In the freezing north winds the little brother was wearing only a flour sack. Early next morning Mike and I pulled back the tarp over the top of the big truck and dug into the boxes of clothing. It wasn't long until that shivering little girl and her brother were warmly clothed, from hoods to shoes, with clothes that had once kept American children warm. As we looked into those two happy orphan faces, we saw smiles that silver and gold cannot buy. I think Jesus was pleased as he watched. I could almost hear him say, "I was hungry and you gave me food. I was naked and you gave me clothes." Little wonder this orphan girl wanted us to take them with us. How frightening was the storm around their lonely, homeless little hearts!

Distributing relief clothing also helped prepare the way for the preaching of the gospel. When people saw that we were sharing American clothes with the cold and needy, young and old, they realized that the message of Jesus Christ means business, that it is not just a message of empty words.

Newborn Christians in Korea feel that they have been saved to serve. They gladly take part in the services. In many churches where there is no regular preacher, the deacons preach and lead in their church work.

Fred and Tom, two GIs who were soldiering for the Lord as well as for Uncle Sam, started the first Royal Ambassador chapter ever organized in Korea, with ten boys in the First Baptist Church in Pusan. It wasn't long until their membership of ten grew to 125. Among this number was Prince Lee, who would have become emperor of Korea, had the order of things continued. The *RA Manual* was translated into Korean. As these Baptist boys took their Bibles and manuals to other parts of Korea, new RA chapters sprang up. (Shortly before Mrs. Ray and I left Korea in 1956, the RAs in Seoul organized a Baptist Brotherhood.)

When the girls saw what the boys were doing, they asked, "Isn't there something for girls, too?" And soon a Girl's

Auxiliary was organized and its members were working enthusiastically for Jesus.

One night two GAs brought a five-year-old girl to my living quarters at Pum Il Dong Baptist Church. They had found her in the gutter in Pusan, and at first had thought she was dead. The little specimen of suffering humanity was covered with dirt and grime, her hair a tangled mat. I got out clean clothes, soap, washcloths, and towels, and told the girls to bathe her. When they returned, their little rescued one was clean, washed, combed, and dressed in clean clothes. But her face was still bloated and her stomach empty. My cook set out some food for the starving waif, and she was soon well filled. The cook and the pastor's family fixed a bed for her— perhaps the first she had slept in for more than a year. Early next morning, the GA girls were back. They had found an orphanage willing to take her in. There was happiness all around!

The Korean Baptist Convention was growing. John Abernathy's 1954 annual report showed that nearly two thousand redeemed people had followed Christ in baptism. There were forty Woman's Missionary Societies with two thousand members. Young people in RAs and GAs did much witnessing for Jesus. Eager to further expand the work, they sent urgent invitations for Southern Baptists to send more missionaries.

Jesus approved of rest, for he went alone into the mountains to seek refreshment of body and soul. Since I had preached over most of South Korea and had driven over many thousands of miles of Korea's stony highways and country trails in relief and evangelistic work, it seemed best for me to seek rest in the U. S. A. This I did.

# 12
# Korea, Last Term

Back home, enjoying a pleasant meal with my boyhood friend, Dr. Will Fleming, of Fort Worth, Texas, he asked me if there was something I would like to take back with me to Korea.

He became the donor of a new jeep and trailer, which were soon loaded with clothes and other supplies. Again I headed for Korea, via Texas, New Mexico, Arizona, and California. At San Francisco I boarded a freighter to cross the Pacific Ocean once more.

"Bye-bye, Janet, my darling partner. I'll hope to see you soon in Korea. This is likely my last journey for Jesus to the mission field, so I must hurry on before the sun gets too low for me to see the many tasks that await my coming."

What a very happy welcome I received as our ship pulled alongside the wharf in Pusan. In that throng of Korean Christian friends and missionaries was my tall missionary boy, Daniel B., and his smiling wife, Frances Jean. (When my work is all done here on earth, I hope to be standing with the happy throng on that other shore when Dan and Jeanie anchor their bark.)

106

Ashore, the customs permitted the Will Fleming jeep to proceed through the streets of Pusan to the Baptist Mission. Having passed our many barrels of relief clothing through customs, we rolled them into place in the mission's front yard, where some twenty GA girls gladly began unpacking the clothes that had been packed by other Girl's Auxiliary members in Texas.

Hope revived and my soul was happy to be again on the highways of Korea for the Lord. Silas Park, a fine university graduate who had been a Christian for about a year, was my new assistant. He had not yet learned to drive a car, so I had to do all the driving for awhile.

As we went, preaching and distributing relief clothing and food, we saw many of our Korean brethren in country churches. It was encouraging to see my big boy Dan and Ted Dowell as they shouldered the responsibilities of building and conducting the new Baptist seminary in Taejon. Our hearts were also thrilled at the sight of the beautiful new stone church building that Brother Abernathy was helping to build in Seoul. Seventy-five Baptist army chaplains in Korea made this possible. Months soon rolled into history.

Happy day it was when I met Mrs. Ray in Japan and escorted her via airplane to Korea. In Japan Dr. and Mrs. Frank Connely did much to make our short visit with them a happy one. Little did we know that this was to be our last visit on earth with him, for God had him on the sailing list for the heavenly city ere long.

On our way from Seoul to Pusan by train, Mrs. Ray and I stopped off and spent a happy Christmas with Dan and Jeanie and our first grandson, Mark, on his first Christmas.

In Pusan, our living quarters were rooms over one corner of the church building, on the noisy main street. It was either this or a place on the sidewalks with the beggars. Across the street from the church was a bus station. Their idea of securing more passengers was to make more and louder noise with the horns and loudspeakers on the front end of their many busses. The loud horns were pointed right at our church, and especially at the corner where we lived. These noises began at four o'clock in the morning and continued until shortly before midnight. These were the most nerve-wracking experiences of our thirty-six years on the mission fields.

Mrs. Ray was a great help to me in handling the relief clothing. She also gave much help to Korean mothers. Her great faith helped keep me going in the biggest task ahead of us. When I left Texas the last time, I had hoped to give my full time to evangelistic work in Korea. Little did I know what really lay ahead.

The mission had begun construction of the Baptist hospital in Pusan. Dr. Hayward had started the basement of one wing, then he returned to America. The executive committee of the mission and the Foreign Mission Board asked me to undertake completion of this building.

Long hours of figuring, planning, hunting materials, battling with import customs officials, exercising super-patience with workmen—then seasoning it all with tears and prayer were needed to build a Baptist hospital of stone, steel, and concrete in war-wasted Korea. But when we had once set our hearts, hands, and heads to the task, there was no turning back until it was complete.

Bighearted American soldiers and sailors gave us a boost where we needed it—in the pocketbook. They gave us twenty-five thousand dollars. Then, too, we received a great deal of extra help and technical advice from the officers and men of the army. The three-story building is one of the strongest buildings in the city of Pusan. Only the devil and the Russians could destroy it, and even then not unless our God is willing. The hospital not only has rooms and places for healing and caring for the sick but also a beautiful chapel.

There seemed to be only one name for this magnificent house of healing—Wallace Memorial Baptist Hospital. I feel greatly humbled that our Lord permitted me to serve for fourteen years in China with that great soldier of the cross— Dr. William L. Wallace, from Knoxville, Tennessee. During the Japanese blockade of China, Dr. Wallace kept open the Stout Memorial Hospital at Wuchow. A great surgeon, doctor, and deacon, he loved the Chinese people and they loved him to the end. It was through the impact of a battering ram that Dr. Wallace's gentle spirit went home to be with his Lord.

With happy hearts, Mrs. Ray and I handed over the keys of the new hospital—the only one Southern Baptists have in Korea —to Dr. N. A. Bryan and nurses Lucy Wright, Ruby Wheat, and Irene Branum.

The burning desire of my soul was finally to be realized. Sam Park, a singing witness of the Lord, joined me in my last work in Korea—preaching in the country churches. Our jeep took us from Pusan in the south to Seoul at the north, Kunsan of the west coast to Pohang on the eastern shores of that beloved needy land.

One night in Pusan there was a knock on our door. A young Baptist preacher escorted into our crowded little living-dining-reception room a young Korean woman about twenty-three years old. Her hair was tangled; her clothes were torn, ragged, and dirty. Her face and hands were scratched with dried bloody marks, showing that she had been in a battle of some kind. The young preacher told us her sad story.

When the multitudes had fled south from Seoul, ahead of pursuing Communists, this young woman was lost from her family. She joined other girls in the Korean Army to help her country in its struggle against the Reds. However, Korean soldiers took advantage of her beauty and tried to drag her down. She fled to the police for protection but they were no better. They put her in a hotel, and there she had fought them with all her strength, for she was a Christian. This was her condition when the young preacher found her, miserable and homeless; so he brought her to us. Mrs. Ray got her some warm clothes, and we put her in a good hotel nearby for the night. The next day we took her to a friendly orphanage that we had been helping. They agreed to keep her until we could find a home for her.

My assistant was so wrought up by the disgraceful conduct of soldiers and police of Korea that he called a news reporter and gave him the whole story. After the paper was published, there came another knock on our door. A well-dressed young woman entered, with a well-cared-for baby strapped on her back. She said that she saw in the paper the account of the unfortunate young woman's terrible experience and she believed the young woman was her sister. She was taken to the orphanage, but kept out of sight until she saw the girl first. When she saw that it really was her own sister, she jumped out of the jeep and, in the presence of the other women and orphans, the two sisters fell into each other's arms and wept for joy. There was more happy news for the rescued sister: "Our mother is alive and lives near here!" Jesus had knocked at our door in the form of a suffering, friendless girl. We were happy he could say, "I was a stranger and ye took me in, I was hungry and ye gave me something to eat, naked and ye gave me clothes to put on."

As Brother Sam and I visited Baptist churches in cities, along the highways, and even in the mountains, my heart went out to these faithful children of God—and especially to the unsaved, knowing that we would see each other no more. Everywhere we told the Christians, "May our Lord richly bless and keep you safe. We shall see you again, the next time in our Father's house beyond the skies. Good-bye, brothers and sisters, till we meet again."

Many years and miles were far behind. The three-score-and-ten milepost had been passed, when a message came from Dr. Baker J. Cauthen, secretary of the Foreign Mission Board: "Brother Ray, it's now time to come home. I hope you will take it as a call of the Lord to come and give the rest of your years speaking, stirring the hearts of our people for foreign missions and relief, and locating young people for future missionaries." That was what I had wanted to do when the Lord first called me to preach, but he had said, "Go." Forty-eight years later, my heart's desire was to stay in Korea to the end of life's journey, but the command was, "Come home." There is always one answer: "Lord, thy will be done."

The other missionaries—preachers, teachers, doctors, and nurses—already had more than they could do. I was the only one trying to give full time to country evangelistic work. Should I fold up my little tent and steal silently away? Was no one to take over this urgent task of taking the gospel into the highways and byways of South Korea?

We felt we could not leave until replacement came. It was a happy hour, one very cold morning in January, when a big freight ship slipped quietly alongside the wharf in Pusan, with the answer to our prayers—Brother and Sister Parkes Marler and their little girl. With our Korean friends, we gave them the grandest welcome we knew how. Hearts at ease, we were now ready to pack up and fly very far away.

# 13

# Grandparents to Orphans

As our eyes and thoughts turned toward faraway Texas, a little red-headed orphan boy, Johnny, was placed in our hands. Leave him behind in Korea? No, we couldn't do that. One morning a Korean man brought little three-year-old, brown-eyed Junie and left her in Mrs. Ray's lap. Leave her behind in Korea? No, never! Too, there was little cotton-topped Timothy, nearly starving in an orphanage. Surely we must take him.

Then came the husbandless mothers of Jackie, dimple-cheeked Jeanie, chubby little Alta Lynn, smiling and worried Joy Ann, round-eyed Jimmy, smiling and very hopeful Sandra, and baby Christine. These mothers begged us to take their GI children with us and find homes for them in America. Yes, we will take all of them. Other little GI orphans we located also—among them, one sad little girl who became the adopted daughter of Roy and Dale Rogers in California.

I must tell you about Mary Kim, seven years old, in Miss Rowe's orphanage in Kunsan. She came to live with us six months before we left Pusan. Being very bright, under Mrs. Ray's guidance, she rapidly learned to speak English. She, too, was anxious to find a home in America and someone to call "Mother." She found her home with Mr. and Mrs. A. L. Lusby in Paris, Texas.

Several weeks dragged by as I filled out papers, papers, and still more papers for the U. S. and Korean governments. In addition to all the questionnaires and adoption papers, there were the hospitals to be satisfied. They used various needles on us and the kiddies. Some of the needles pumped in medicine and others sucked out blood for various tests. Before we got through, some of our little ones got needle-nurse-and-doctor-shy, and for painful reasons. After weeks of this torture, we came out of the last doctor's office into the sunshine. Little red-top Johnny smiled away his tears as I carried him along in my arms, and he began singing a baby tune.

Before we could leave Korea, however, Alta Lynn's own mother, who had signed release papers for her to be adopted in America, kidnapped her dimple-cheeked baby and sold her to another Korean woman. Sam and I searched frantically everywhere. Finally I enlisted the services of the U. S. Army CID (similar to U. S. FBI). One Sunday morning just as I was ready to go into the pulpit to preach in the Pusan First Baptist Church, the CID GI drove his jeep into our churchyard and asked me to come quickly. He had located the place, miles away, where Alta Lynn was held, and he would escort me to it. He had left one of his men on guard, lest the baby should be spirited away. Miss Kim Han Hee, who later went to our WMU Training School in Louisville, Kentucky, jumped into my jeep, and we followed the GI and his assistant in his jeep. When we got to the house where the baby was, the GI said that he had done all he could do and it was up to me from there on.

The woman who had bought the baby stood on the front porch in a defiant attitude. Miss Kim spoke firmly and courageously, telling her that we had come to get the baby and meant to take her with us. I told the woman that she could take her choice—give us that baby or go to prison at once, because the baby was no longer a Korean but an American, as she had been legally adopted. Finally, neighbor women standing by told the woman that she had better let Pastor Ray take the baby away. She relented and had the baby brought out. I don't know where they had her in the back room, but when they brought the little thing out, her cheeks were covered with tears and she had bites all over her face and arms, either from bedbugs or mosquitoes.

Our worries were not over. About two days before our departure by air from Seoul, the mother of Jean Ann stole and hid her. We postponed our flying date and got the police in Seoul and the Korean police in Pusan to search both cities for the stolen girl. I rushed back to Pusan, where Sam and I joined the frantic search. Jean Ann, too, had been legally adopted in America, her passport had been issued, and her plane ticket purchased. Even her flying clothes were ready. But for once I had to admit defeat. With sad hearts, we prepared to fly. Our faith in God had not failed, though, and we prayed that he would move the heart of that mother to return little Jean Ann to us. The Lord answered our prayers, and the mother did bring Jeannie to our friend Sam and his mother in Pusan. Sam took her back to Seoul and put her in care of Brother and Sister Raetz, who were caring for our other kiddies while final papers were being approved. She joined the others who came on a later plane.

When our latest flying date arrived, Brother Marler took Mrs. Ray and me out to the children's home. Our six little fellow passengers were hurriedly dressed in their nicest "relief" clothes for the flight to the new homes that anxiously awaited them beyond the seas.

With Johnny and Alta Lynn in our arms, Jackie, Timmy, "Skinny Girl," and our little colored girl in tow, we found our seats on the plane. Soon we were securely bound in our seats with heavy belts, ready for the take-off. Jackie and Tim didn't like having their personal liberty tied down like that, but their vociferous objections were soon drowned out by the sputtering motors.

Our big four-engined Northwest Orient Airliner roared out across Seoul, and slowly the mountain peaks of Korea faded into the distance and were seen no more. The Sea of Japan glided beneath us, and then Japan with its mountains and rice fields and a big airfield at Tokyo. There, after a few hours of inspections and waiting, we boarded our plane again and soared above the mountains and seas toward the Aleutian Islands of Alaska.

About two hours after sunrise, when we were flying four miles high at 350 miles an hour above the sea of clouds, our pilot announced, "We are going to land." The plane nose-dived into dark clouds. Darker and darker they became as down and down we went. With seat belts buckled tightly, we roared to a stop amidst fog, mist, and ice. After refueling, again we ascended into the blue skies, and all day and part of the night we heard only the roar of the four big engines. It is far more comforting to hear *four* engines, than *three* out of four, as had happened once when I winged across the Pacific.

After dark, thousands of sparkling blue, red, and other bright lights appeared beneath us. It's America! It's Seattle! ! ! Once on the earth again, we and our six hangers-on dragged and pushed through chutes and corridors. Bags, passports, and many papers for the children were "goggled at" by various sizes and dispositions of customs officials doing their duty. After hours of patience-testing questions by officials and having rescued Jackie several times from his self-appointed tours to see America first for himself, we were hustled into a smaller crowded airplane on our way to Los Angeles. I sat folded

into a chair, with Tim across my lap and his head hooked
into my left arm. Another small fry was lying across Tim and
that one's head hooked into my right arm. In another chair
Mrs. Ray was carrying double also. Thus we sweated it out
as we flew on toward San Francisco. When the plane rolled
safely to a stop, a portly woman and her three chubby off-
spring got off the plane. So Mom and I came up for air.
Being strapped down with two hefty, tired youngsters buckled
on top of you for hours does not make one shouting happy
about traveling by air!

When we landed in Los Angeles, some well-dressed colored
people from Fort Worth, Texas, rushed and took possession
of our beautiful little colored girl. A Los Angeles couple took
our little skin-and-bones girlie. All the way from Korea to the
U. S. A., she had seemed hungry day and night.

Dr. and Mrs. J. R. Saunders, ex-China missionaries, took us
to their home in Los Angeles, fed us abundantly, and let us
breathe some free American air that was not vibrating with
the sputter and roar of airplane engines. On our way to Dr.
Saunders' home, the sight of hundreds of cars dashing at
high speed up to a red light with a sudden stop, and then
swarms of other cars rushing in both directions through green
lights, made me think that America had really gone wild.

After a few hours of wonderful food, and rest in chairs that
were not hurtling through space miles high in the air, we
returned to the airfield and buckled ourselves down again.
This time we were headed for Texas!

Speed did not bother me, as we sailed far above the mountains and the pillars of snowy clouds. The blue, hazy mountains in southern California, the sandy, sizzling deserts of
Arizona, and the lone prairies of New Mexico and western
Texas brought a feeling of quietness and peace to our excited
hearts. Fields, fences, and houses came into view beneath us,
and a comforting feeling stole into our beings that before long

our journey halfway around the world would be ended. Yes, we were "headin' for home" in Texas.

The smoky city of Dallas heaved into view, and our plane poked her nose into the feed trough at the home ranch. I wobbled down the gangway with Johnny and Jackie in my arms, as Mrs. Ray followed with Alta Lynn strapped on her back, Chinese style, and towing Tim by the hand. Cameras of all kinds and sizes were whirring and snapping at us, as flashbulbs dazzled our eyes. We met them head-on and face to face. Smiles and handshaking and greetings let us know that our almost sleepless flight out of war-torn Korea was over!

"You pops and moms, here are your new Americans," we said. "Come, take 'em into your arms and love 'em as we do."

Our own children, together with the fathers and mothers of their newly arrived babies, soon rescued us from news reporters, camera bugs, and goggle-eyed friends. They rushed us into their waiting cars. At the home of the Reids in Richardson, a bountiful feast awaited us on their velvety lawn. Sitting there in a comfortable chair, I began to tell my daughter Mary Dee and my nephew Claude Earl Hicks about my journey, but soon fell asleep talking. Several times I awoke, to see them laughing at me for trying to talk and sleep at the same time!

Thanks and praise to my Pilot for the many trails he led me safely over since I signed a contract for life with the Foreign Mission Board in September, 1919. All glory and praise forever to Jesus Christ who saved me in 1905, called me to be a missionary preacher in 1908, and released me from service in the mission field of Korea in 1956. I hope to do his will to the end of the long, long trail.

This account was finished beside rippling, cold waters, among the towering fir and spruce trees in the mountains east of Seattle, Washington, September 2, 1957.

# Epilogue

(Written by Rex Ray's daughter, Mrs. Lois McKenzie, the following was inspired and approved by him and contains his last public utterance, the prayer that moved a town.)

A telegram on New Year's Day, 1958—a greeting, no doubt from our son, from the army camp. Just yesterday was his birthday.

"With deep regret I inform you. . . ." No! This is peacetime! Soldiers are not being killed these days. There must be a mistake! "Died after being hit by a motor vehicle."

But, Lord, how can it be? He was so vigorous and happy a few short weeks ago as he waved good-bye from the train. But death is death, whether in savage battle or in the merry-making mayhem of holiday traffic. Yet—praise the Lord— death need not be final.

"I am the resurrection and the life." How often I have preached this message during fifty years in his service. Help me, Lord, to realize now its full meaning.

"All things work together for good to them that love God." Father, how can that really be? Our first-born son, still young,

118

re-enlisting after nine years of service in two wars, and training at last for the work he had always wanted to do. Why, Lord, would it happen now? Humanly speaking, there is, I suppose, no really *good* time to die. But then, your Son was a young man too, at the very prime of life. Help us, O Lord, to understand and to accept. Help us to see beyond these human tears of tragedy that "death is swallowed up in victory."

How deep and warm is Christian sympathy! The friendly visits and telephone calls, lovely flowers, the comforting letters and cards—our feeling of appreciation all but overwhelms us. We are amazed at the number of our son's friends and are encouraged by the thoughtfulness of people, some whom we do not even know. Yet there remains the heartache and the wondering query, "Why?"

Three days and several long distance telephone calls later, another yellow envelope comes to our door: "The remains of your son, the late Private First Class David F. Ray, are being shipped at government expense, escorted by Private First Class Donald R. Irvin." Funeral arrangements proceed smoothly, and Pfc. Irvin courteously delivers his charge.

It is not easy, Lord, to bury one's firstborn. We had such hopes for his future! But you, too, know this heartache. Give us the grace to bear it and the vision to see thy purpose in it all. May thy Spirit guide us through this "valley of the shadow" and use our sorrow to thy glory.

But, Lord, what is this you ask of me? I feel thy Spirit's impression, and yet . . . to lead in prayer at my own son's funeral when my heart is broken—it seems unusual, Lord. But you have often asked me to do the unusual. Give me the strength to witness again to thy love.

In the solemn hush of the funeral home, sympathetic friends and sorrowing loved ones join us before the quiet form of our son, lying there in the sleep of death. An array of battle ribbons and medals adorns his uniform; our nation's flag is draped over him. Restful music begins, and beloved hymns of victory soothe our aching hearts. The service proceeds with quiet dignity.

Promises from thy Book assure us that our David has gone to be with thee. "I have come that they might have life, and that they might have it more abundantly." Now it is my turn. O Lord, steady my voice and my emotions as I pray:

Our Heavenly Father, we come to thee because there is no other to whom we can come in an hour like this. We thank you for all these friends who are not bought with silver and gold. Today we remember yonder in faraway China when David was only a year old and it looked like he was going to leave us, we surrendered our wills to thine and said that you could take him if you wanted to. You let us keep him, but we have never recalled the surrender of our will that you could have him at any time. We thank you for the remembrance of that hour when he and Dan, eight and ten years old, gave their hearts to Christ under the preaching of a Chinese evangelist. We thank you for the hope the boys found that day in Christ that has carried them all the way.

Again we want to thank you for your watchcare over David during his nine years in the army—when his ship exploded at sea, and through the many trips when they brought wounded soldiers back to the U. S. A. We thank you for your special protection over him on the battlefield when he carried in his wounded buddies under fire.

Lord, we thank you for this soldier-boy, Don Irvin, who brought our David home to us. If he is not a Christian, Lord, wilt thou lead him to find Jesus as his Saviour. Today, Lord, we would not forget to pray for the young man who was riding in the car with death when David was struck down. If he was not a Christian, use this experience to lead him to a saving knowledge of Jesus. . . . Comfort the hearts of the loved ones of David's lady companion, whose life was blotted out the same instant.

Lord, we thank thee for these young preachers here today who are helping us. Do set their hearts on fire to preach the gospel as long as they shall live.

Lord, wilt thou bless all these friends and the homes represented here today. May the way grow brighter and brighter for us all until that day when you shall say, "It is enough. Come home."

These things we ask in our Saviour's name. Amen!

Tearfully our friends file by. Thank you, Father, for their concern! Is it time already for the last glimpse of this young soldier, our own flesh and blood? This son with whom we walked the floor, and played, and prayed? My World War I experience as a chaplain comes to the fore, and as I pass his silent form, I can but salute. "Good-bye, Sonny Boy." His mother makes her final tender ministrations—and we see him no more. What now, O Lord?

At the cemetery a military guard stands at attention as the flag-draped casket is borne to its resting place. The chaplain speaks the final rites, "Dust to dust. . . ." Sadly but proudly we accept the folded flag—tribute from "a grateful government." Three volleys ring out and "Taps" is sounded clearly on the cool breeze.`It is over. The physical symbol of our thirty-six years of parenthood is in his grave. But, is this the end?

We have invited Pfc. Irvin ("Don" to us now), our son's comrade-in-arms and final escort, to stay with us until his return to camp the following evening. En route home from the cemetery we learn that his heart has been touched by the funeral events and that he is concerned about his spiritual life. A preacher friend has given him a New Testament. Lord, truly this is thy doing. Make us adequate for the challenge.

A pleasant evening and a long night's rest refresh us all. The next afternoon the Holy Spirit has prepared the setting and moves our hearts as we discuss God's saving grace and the meaning of surrender to him. Don realizes his need, and soon my grandchild's playpen becomes an altar of victory as we kneel before the Lord in prayer. Not long afterward, Don expresses his desire to win his lost father—a convincing evidence of his genuine salvation.

Truly, the work of the Lord is marvelous in our eyes, and his ways past finding out! Out of human bereavement has come divine victory and we sing out with Paul, "O death, where is thy sting? O grave, where is thy victory?" The loss of our son in the flesh has brought us a son in the Lord. Who knows what great things the Master has in store for Don? His quick mind and good voice, his youthful vigor and enthusiasm—only God knows what service he may render. Our prayers are with him. And we realize afresh that all things do "work together for good to them that love God, to them who are the called according to his purpose."

### January, 1958

The cowboy rides in the last roundup, and the missionary warrior reports to the Captain of his soul.

Within three weeks of his son David's funeral, Rex Ray himself entered the heavenly portals which he had long anticipated with much enthusiasm. His lifetime prayer was answered—to be active until the end, for his family had to cancel more than a solid month of speaking engagements when he reported for greater service above.

"It's been a great fight," he said to his good friend Baker James Cauthen, secretary of the Southern Baptist Foreign Mission Board, who visited him shortly before the final battle. The words of another missionary warrior come to mind: "I have fought a good fight, I have finished my course, I have kept the faith" (2 Tim. 4:7).

"It's all over," Rex Ray said at another time and added, "Eternity!" To him the heavenly city was almost in sight. In the words of Robert Browning's "Prospice," he could well have said, "I was ever a fighter, so—one more fight, the best and the last!"

The dread effects of acute leukemia took their toll. The mortal frame remained behind as a loyal subject knelt before his Saviour. During life he had often gone first into war-torn mission fields, preparing the way for his beloved wife to follow. So now he led the way, while her voice sang out in ringing tones the prayer of their triumphant faith—that great hymn by Charles Wesley:

> Jesus, lover of my soul,
>     Let me to Thy bosom fly,
> While the nearer waters roll,
>     While the tempest still is high:
> Hide me, O my Saviour, hide,
>     Till the storm of life is past;
> Safe into the haven guide;
>     O receive my soul at last!

# Date Due

|  |  |  |  |
|---|---|---|---|
|  |  |  |  |
|  |  |  |  |
|  |  |  |  |
|  |  |  |  |
|  |  |  |  |
|  |  |  |  |
|  |  |  |  |
|  |  |  |  |
|  |  |  |  |
|  |  |  |  |
|  |  |  |  |
|  |  |  |  |
|  |  |  |  |
|  |  |  |  |
|  |  |  |  |
|  |  |  |  |
|  |  |  |  |
|  |  |  |  |
|  |  |  |  |
|  |  |  |  |

Code 4386-04, CLS-4, Broadman Supplies, Nashville, Tenn.,
Printed in U.S.A.